The Island Dog Squad
(Book 3: People Problems)
By Deb McEwan

The right of Deb McEwan to be identified as the author of this work has been asserted by her in accordance with the Copyright, Designs and Patents Act 1988.

This is a work of fiction. While some places and events are a matter of fact, the characters are the product of the author's imagination and are used in a fictitious manner. Any resemblance to actual persons, living or dead, is purely coincidental.

(c) Copyright Deb McEwan 2018

Cover Design by Jessica Bell

"Dogs leave pawprints on our hearts"
Author Unknown

Prologue

He didn't know this was to be his final day when he heard voices.

Henry had plenty of time to contemplate his actions. Chained up in a single pen, Steve had done everything he could think of to train him during the dog's stay at the rescue centre, but it had been useless. True to character, Henry snarled and attempted to attack both the four-legged inhabitants and the two-legged staff and helpers.

'I hate it when it comes to this but I've tried everything. He's one of the few unresponsive dogs I've ever had the misfortune to meet,' Steve said to the vet.

The visitor patted his arm. 'It's unfortunate, Steve, but it's not the dog's fault. He's had too much cruelty and aggression in his life. I was hoping for a miracle but didn't really expect you to be able to do anything. This one is too far gone.'

Henry growled as the men approached. Steve opened the cage and gripped the dog, stopping him from moving. Even within the constraints of his chain Henry struggled and attempted to free himself.

'You poor, sad boy,' Steve said. 'What a miserable life you've led.' He turned to the vet. 'Imagine never being shown any love or kindness, where your one and only job is to hurt anyone or anything that crosses your path? No wonder he's mad.'

As the vet administered the lethal injection, Henry now knew his owner wasn't coming for him. In a lucid moment prior to his death, he realised his one purpose in life was to frighten all other living beings. He had never been loved, or even liked. He made one pitiful, painful howl against all the injustices in his sad life, before sinking into painless unconsciousness.

The day Henry was put down, his owner, Michaelis, appeared in court on charges of animal cruelty.

'I find you guilty as charged,' said the judge, 'and sentence you to six months in prison, suspended for two years. If you appear before me again within that period, you will go down. Furthermore, your licence to own any animals is revoked.' He banged his gavel and stood.

'All rise,' called the court usher.

As the judge left, a look passed between Michaelis and his twin brother, Yanni. Their thoughts were mirrored and they didn't need words. Top of the list was revenge on those who had put Michaelis in the courtroom, made his ownership of animals illegal and thereby made the twins' other business activities more difficult.

Steve and Panni were sleeping in the small shack adjacent to the rescue centre. One of the dogs was sick and they were taking it in turns to check on her through the night. She seemed to have passed crisis point and had settled, so they both decided to rest for a few hours.

The barking woke Steve, before the acrid smell of smoke, which hit him as soon as he came to his senses. He had no idea of the time, but it was still pitch black - except for the orange flames he could see through the small window.

'What the...?' he shouted, then, 'Panni! Panni!' Panni must have already beein in the process of waking because he jumped off the camp bed in a flash. They were already wearing shorts, so Steve ran out of the door, with Panni hot on his heels.

The sight that greeted them stopped both men in their tracks. The building housing the dogs was engulfed in flames and the terrified barking and wailing coming from inside shocked Steve to the core. He rushed towards the door. Seeing his plan, Panni intervened.

'It's too late, Steve. There's nothing we can do.'

Steve tried desperately to shake him off. 'I've got to try. We can't just leave them.'

There was less noise as each second passed, and the air was soon filled with the smell of burning flesh. Steve headed towards the door despite Panni's protests, but something else got to it before him.

There was an almighty crash and the door hit the ground as a massive dog flew through the air and landed on the floor. He was on fire. Steve rushed to the shack, grabbing the first thing that came to hand. Recognising the dog as Baxter he dived on top of him. The dog was wailing pitifully and the flames were soon extinguished. It was only then Steve noticed the small dog hanging, upside down, from Baxter's belly. She was whimpering. Baxter was still breathing but the two dogs who managed to follow them out had lost their battle, along with those locked inside in their pens. Steve sank to the floor, crying into Baxter's fur as the small dog fell to the floor. He picked her up and held her close, whispering soothing words in an attempt to stop her from shaking.

'It'll be all right, Lexi, you're safe now. Everything's going to be all right.' It was obvious to Panni that Steve didn't believe his own words, and seeing his friend's distress, Panni had trouble holding back his own tears as he phoned the fire brigade and their twenty-four-hour vet.

Chapter 1 – Sandy's Home

It was a Wednesday evening and I was lying by Ben's feet as he watched the footie match. Ellie was in the other room on the computer.

'Look at this, Ben.' I heard her call. I padded into the study behind Ben and watched as she pointed at her screen.

'Are you on Nosey Book again?'

Ellie sighed, ignoring his comment as she pointed to the computer screen. 'Look at this article.'

'The match is on, Ellie. Can't you just tell me... damn...!' he cursed, and we both ran to the living room as a roar came from the television. 'I missed the flaming goal!'

Ben sat on the sofa to watch the goal replay, and I settled at his feet again, once he had finished shouting and jumping up and down.

'I'll come and have a look at half-time,' he called to Ellie.

Not much later, the adverts came on and I trotted behind him into the study again.

'There's an article in The Weekly about the fire, Ben. They said it's definitely arson but they haven't found the person who started it yet.'

'We already knew that, the Fire Chief...'

'Yup,' interrupted Ellie, 'but we didn't know this...' We both watched as she scrolled down her computer screen, opened another page, and started reading out loud.

'Michaelis Savvidis, thirty-eight, was recently convicted of animal cruelty despite denying all charges. The judge imposed a prison sentence of six months, to be suspended for two years. In addition, Savvidis was ordered to pay a fine of five hundred euros and had his licence to hunt and to keep animals revoked.

In an exclusive interview following the case, Yanni Savvidis, the influential twin brother of Michaelis, said the sentencing was outrageous and the family intended to appeal. He added that his brother's reputation was in ruins and, "he did not expect the decision to be upheld when 'lying foreigners' had persecuted his family for years and the judge decided to believe that so-called evidence, instead of the facts of honest working men." Yanni went on to say that they would take it all the way to the European Court of Human Rights if island justice was found wanting.

Meanwhile, in other news, the heatwave continues across the island and the fire risk remains high. Everyone is advised to take care and comply with the regulations about barbecuing in public areas, throwing away rubbish in the countryside and carelessly discarding cigarette ends.'

'Well?'

'Well, indeed,' said Ben. 'He should have been locked up and the key thrown away, along with that scumbag of a brother.'

'But what if he wins the appeal?'

'I think it's all bluff, Ellie. His ego's bruised and it's a heat of the moment reaction. It would be a waste of money appealing against such a small fine and sentence, and if what that police sergeant said is true, it could draw attention to their other illegal activities.'

'Do you think we've heard the last of them?'

'Of course.' Ben put an arm around Ellie and gave her a reassuring kiss on the cheek.

'Second half is about to start... and don't believe everything you read on there,' he nodded towards the screen before making his way back into the living room.

As I followed Ben, I didn't believe it was the last we would hear of the twins, any more than they did.

Chapter 2

It was the weekend; Saturday evening to be precise, and change was afoot yet again.

I was sitting outside with the folks who had completed all of their chores and were in a particularly light-hearted mood. I couldn't say the same about my mine. In a few days' time when the folks were at work, I was to meet with Lola, Obie, and Chip, at Tulip's home. Unfortunately, it wasn't to plan a mission or just to hang out. It was a farewell to Tulip, whose family were leaving and we would never see him again. I'd become used to having him around; he was a good friend, as well as a valued member of our dog squad.

'Come on, Ben,' said Ellie, 'you have a go.'

They'd distracted me and I watched as Ellie juggled three mandoras, or should I say attempted to juggle, I corrected myself. One of the orange fruits dropped to the floor and split. It was too sweet for me so I remained lying down instead of pouncing on the dropped food as I usually did before one of them could pick it up.

They both stopped what they were doing and looked at me. 'What's the matter, eh, girl?' Ben asked, and I sighed and put my head on my paws.

'I think she's depressed.'

'Dogs don't get depressed, Ellie,' Ben replied. 'Come on, Sandy. Let's see if we can find you a tastier treat.'

Good idea, Ben. As it was the weekend, I hoped it would be a special treat. I wasn't disappointed and put Tulip out of my head for a while as I chewed on the tasty meat inside the delicious marrow bone.

'See, she's just fine.'

'She's not her usual self, Ben. Dogs might not get depressed but I'm telling you that Sandy's not happy.'

I hardly noticed when Ben's, *'Yes dear,'* was met with a sharp squeeze to his thigh that made him cry out.

Then nature took its course and before I could help myself, Ellie started fanning her hand in front of her face, and looked at me.

'Eww, Sandy, that stinks, you dirty dog.'

I needed a bit of fun to try to lighten my mood so I looked pointedly at Ben, then sighed and lay down.

'Ben?'

'No way, Ellie. I'm not taking the blame for that.'

'Oh come on, Ben! Be a man, you can't blame Sandy for everything.'

'But it wasn't...'

'It's all right, Sandy,' she said as she walked towards me. 'I believe you.'

Thankfully their exchange had taken a little time and the smell had now disappeared. When Ben looked at me with raised eyebrows, I winked at him. It was the first time he seemed to cotton on to the fact that I was actually capable of such deviousness and he looked suitably confused.

Any further looks from Ben were temporarily ignored as I revelled in Ellie's kisses and cuddles, forcing myself to live in the moment and feeling better for doing so.

We walked to Tulip's house from different directions the following Monday morning, not wanting to travel in a pack and draw attention to ourselves. Saying that, the three people I saw on the journey were in their own little worlds, tapping away at their electronic devices, and none of them noticed me anyway - phones do that to people. Then again, it could also be because it was a Monday, which generally puts people in strange moods. I was the first to arrive and Tulip and I reminisced about the times we'd shared, both good and bad.

'I wonder what became of Henry? Do you think rehab worked?'

'Not a chance.' I was no expert in these matters but Henry was pure crazy-evil, and not even the highly-talented and clever Steve-the-Cheese would be able to do anything with that one, never mind how much cheddar he had in his pockets.

'I'm inclined to agree with you, Fish... sorry, *Sandy*. Force of habit when I'm thinking about missions.'

'No problemo, Tulip. I know....' I was interrupted mid-flow by a very distinctive bark.

'Sandee, have you heard the news about Steve-the-Cheeseeee.'

Obie came sprinting into the garden ahead of Chip, which was unusual, and Lola was bringing up the rear.

'What news? What's happened?'

'Lola said it's all over the island...'

'Okay, Obie, that's enough, old chap. Calm down and I'll explain exactly what's happened.'

We were all silenced and forgot for a moment that we were here to say goodbye to Tulip as we prepared to listen to Lola.

'It's very sad I'm afraid, so prepare yourselves for frightfully bad news.'

She'd already had our full attention, so now, instead of relaxing, I was worried and so was Tulip. Chip ran into the garden, picked up on the atmosphere and started to become agitated. He began spinning like he was in a state-of-the-art washing machine, and barking as if the world was coming to an end. Which for some, it already had.

'Enough!' It was one of the loudest barks I'd heard from Lola and it did the trick. We all sat to attention and waited.

'There was a fire in Steve's rescue centre. It's been...'

'What?Where?How?Arethedogs okay? Anyonehurt? Whataboutthe...' Chip was spinning out of control again, so Lola was forced to shout to regain his attention.

'I know this is difficult to hear, old chap, but do calm down and let me speak.'

She waited patiently for Chip to respond, which took a few minutes but felt like a lifetime to me. We all wanted to know what had happened, and most importantly, if there were any casualties.

'I'm afraid it's very bad news...' She closed her eyes for a second, then quietly said, 'there were thirty-five dogs but only two survivors.'

'For the love of Lassie,' I said out loud. My legs went from beneath me and I found myself lying down and covering my head with my front paws. I had no idea how the others reacted, but I just wanted the world to go away. How could this have happened?

'Steve-the-Cheese and his deputy, Panni, were sleeping in an adjacent building and were woken by the fire. Despite their best efforts, only two dogs - Baxter, a big South-African Ridgeback, and Lexi, a small Maltese - survived. It was too dangerous for the men to go in but Baxter's strength saved them both.'

'How are they?' I sat up to ask the question, hoping the poor things were going to be all right.

'Traumatised, as you may well imagine, but Lexi is doing better than Baxter who sustained some burns. She was attached to his undercarriage so suffered smoke inhalation. From what I can glean, they think a flame damaged his neck and he has to keep it covered.'

We waited while Lola appeared to be lost in thought. After a few seconds she added, 'But my sources say they're going to be okay, physically that is I can't imagine one would ever get over this sort of trauma, and I would certainly worry for the big fellow's mental health, and the young lady's.'

None of us spoke as we wondered about the horror the poor dogs had endured before their untimely deaths. Death would have been a release, I imagined, but had probably not come quickly enough.

Lola broke the silence after a while. 'So what's already a sad day has been made even worse.' She turned to

Tulip. 'I say, old chap, I'm terribly sorry to put the dampers on your farewell, but it would have been remiss of me not to share this dreadful news.'

'I understand completely, love,' said Tulip. 'It's a sad day already and I don't want to leave, but I have no choice in the matter. To be fair, I will enjoy the company of the grandchildren, especially now they're a little older and hopefully won't pull on my tail or insist on rides around the house.'

We tried to keep the conversation light, but the news of the fire and so many deaths was hovering in the background like a sinister storm cloud. Well, that's how I felt about it. And I was pretty sure that Lola's thoughts about the whole thing were pretty much in sync with mine.

We had a bit of a run around the garden and nuzzled and sniffed for a while, but our hearts weren't in it so we lay in companionable silence until the sun moving over the horizon signalled that Tulip's people parents would be back before long, and so would the rest of ours.

Lola cleared her throat and nodded and we all sat up and paid attention.

'Tulip, you started as an honorary member of our squad before becoming as fully involved as the rest of us. It's no exaggeration to say that without your help we wouldn't have been able to catch the crazy Henry and have him dealt with. I will be eternally grateful to you and will miss you, as I know we all will.'

'I'm so sorry I won't be here to help in future,' said Tulip. 'I'm going to miss you all, more so than you can ever imagine.'

'We'll miss you too,' I said. 'It won't be the same without you.'

'We wish you the very best of luck and happiness for the future,' said Lola. 'You will always be in our thoughts and hearts, and will be a member of this elite squad in spirit, if not in body.'

It was emotional as we nuzzled and said our final farewells before departing.

We were all subdued on the way to our respective homes and Lola decided to share her thoughts about recent events.

'The fire where Obie's sister so tragically died was proved to be started by despicable arsonists. I have my suspicions, and so do the humans - and trust me, there is absolutely no way that this one was an accident. I consider it the dog squad's responsibility, nay, our duty, to find out who did this and to play our part in bringing them to justice.'

'I'm in,' I said, trying to put my fear onto the back burner.

'and meeee.'

'Whateverittakes.'

'Good. These are dangerous people and dangerous times and it certainly won't be easy.'

Nothing was ever easy, but for Obie to feel safe again we had to somehow ensure his dog nappers came to justice this time. I certainly felt all of these events were linked, though I hadn't yet voiced my suspicions. Lola was so much cleverer than me, so she must have made the connection too. As for Obie and Chip – I had no intention of worrying them until it was absolutely necessary and I figured Lola would be barking up the same tree as far as that was concerned.

We said our goodbyes as we headed different ways through the bondu, in the direction of our own respective homes.

None of us were aware that the future for one of our squad was anything but bright.

Chapter 3

The death of the dogs and destruction of Steve's Rescue Centre was all over Social Media during the next few weeks. Other than that, life was pretty quiet. On walks with Gina and Ellie, Lola told me she was still in the process of devising a plan to find and catch those responsible.

'This isn't going to be easy, Sandy,' she said. 'My Intelligence shows these people have a base some distance away, as well as a house in this village, so I have to find a way for us to get there, or enlist some help.'

The only way I could think of was to hide in a vehicle, and I told her so.

'There's more than one way to skin a cat. I would much rather this be out in the open, old girl.'

'I don't understand, Lola. What does that mean?' I was curious but she said she was unable to share anything further.

'As soon as I have a plan, I'll let you know. Patience, Fish.'

As the days passed, the brown areas turned to green as the drought of the summer ended. Early autumn and late spring were my favourite times of year; late sunrises meant cool morning walks with Ben, but it was pleasant to be able to lie outside in the sunshine during the afternoon or early evening without the intense heat of summer draining all of my mental and physical energy. The nights were chilly enough to sleep without having to walk around the house looking for the cool spots, or the irritation of the air conditioning units that Ellie insisted be switched on. The insects loved her, so as soon as dusk approached she either cloaked herself in a spray that she hoped would make her invisible, or closed all the windows and doors. Sometimes she did both. If we sat outside during the evenings when they didn't have work the following day, she generally wore long trousers (unless she'd had too many of her own drinks), and the occasional Sandy Sour when bravado took over.

This was one of those evenings.

'You know you'll regret it tomorrow, Ellie,' said Ben. I noticed the face she pulled behind his back when he went to refresh the drinks, and smirked to myself. Ben returned with them, put them on the table and took Ellie's cloaking spray out of his shorts pocket.

'Oh, thanks, darling,' she called after him as he went to fill my bowl with fresh water. I'd just finished fishing out the meat from inside a marrow-bone so it was perfect timing.

It was quiet, except for the music playing on their machine. *It's all so beautiful, like a landscape painting in the sky...* the words rang out and Ellie sighed.

'Do you think he knew he was dying when he wrote that?'

'I guess he must have, but we'll never know...'

I had no idea what they were talking about and Ben stopped abruptly as a noise made us all turn and look towards the gate. Any thoughts of further pondering the haunting music disappeared as Obie bounded towards me, with Lola in his wake Gina and her teenage daughter, Laura, briought up the rear. I noticed something different about Gina straight away - she seemed to have more bounce in her step and her energy had changed.

'Wine, gin, or a Sandy Sour?' Ellie asked Gina, and they all laughed. I missed the joke but Laura stopped laughing when her mother told her she could only have a soft drink.

Settled with their glasses, I was the first to notice the smug look on Gina's face, closely followed by Ellie.

'Go on then, spill the beans.'

'I don't know what you mean,' Gina acted coy but Laura put a stop to that.

'Mum's dating Steve the dog man,' she said. 'He's moved into the house near where those two mad twins live. The ones who had the nasty Rottweiler.'

So that's why Gina was different. I went off to play with Obie and Lola to get more information.

'I wondered if anyone had moved into Tulip's homeeee,' Obie whispered, as I nuzzled his neck. 'I went wandering when the gate was open and wondered if anyone had moved into Tulip's place. Steve-the-Cheese found me in his garden when he came home. He gave me some cheese and brought me back.'

'How did he know where you live?'

'He put my photo into a group on the computer. Laura saw it, contacted him and told him. He got chatting with Gina and they've been out a few times sinceeee. She's more relaxed and it's as if he's been around for ever.'

'Tell Sandy about the dogs, old chap.' Lola had been listening quietly until now.

'Baxter's massive, Sandeee, and looks pretty scary when you first see him. The other one is a cute fluffy girl but she seems to be the toughest. They're both traumatised and are inseparable but the big dog isn't well and I feel sorry for him.'

'What do you mean "not well"?'

'What Obie means, old girl, is that as well as having horrific burn marks from that awful fire, the poor chap is anxious and his nerves are on edge.'

'He jumped when a leaf rustled in the garden and it took ages for me to convince him to talk to me and that I wasn't going to hurt him. Lexi the little one, had to reassure him. Can you imagine that, Sandee? A big dog like that thinking *I* could hurt him, or anyone elseeee!'

'No I can't. He must be in a bad way, the poor thing.'

'Understatement, I should say,' said Lola. 'The good news is that both Baxter and Lexi are having the best support possible from Steve, and one can only hope that they will improve a little each day. I think she'll be fine as long as she's around Baxter, but we need to spend time with them both, especially Baxter, to help with his recovery.'

'I can't imagine he could be one of our squad,' I said to Lola. 'Not in his current condition.'

'That's not going to happen, Sandy. This is a mission of kindness, to do whatever we can to make the big chap's life easier. Hopefully, in time he'll be able to forget about the awful things he saw in that fire, and move on with his life.'

'I very much doubt it,' said Obie, and we were all reminded of the hardships he'd endured in his life.

'Do they know those awful twins live in the same village?' I asked.

'No idea,' Lola replied. 'But neither mentioned it to Obie so I very much doubt it. I daresay they'll find out soon enough. But let's not cause any extra anxiety or worry for now, by telling them beforehand. They might not see them, or the twins may actually move. One never can tell.'

I don't know why, but I very much doubted the horrible twins would move. More likely they would want to stay in the village and persecute the people and animals who had upset them. That was a worrying thought process that I didn't want to explore. Thankfully, Ellie's voice put a stop to it.

'Sandy,' she called, as Gina began calling Lola and Obie. Gina rummaged in her bag and dug out three treats. I looked to my people parents, expecting them to say I'd had a bone before the visitors arrived. I knew it would be difficult watching my friends eating if I had to go without.

'Oh, go on then,' said Ben. 'It is the weekend, after all.'

I did a few jumps and twists, copying Chip's behaviour, and the humans laughed. Ben and Ellie were the best people parents ever, I thought. Any further thoughts of Baxter and Lexi or the horrible twins disappeared as I as I got lost in the moment and enjoyed my delicious treat.

Chapter 4

Ben and Ellie were at a wedding on another part of the Island so I was staying at Gina's overnight. As much as I loved Lola and Obie, I would have preferred to have accompanied my human pack.

We played in the garden for hours while Gina ferried the kids to and from various classes. Then, after dinner when it started to get dark, we were all so exhausted we lay in the house by the unlit wood burner. It was still autumn so wasn't cool enough for it to be lit.

Laura had gone out with a friend and Greg was on a sleepover with one of his.

'Gina's looking smart for someone who's staying in on her own,' I remarked to no one in particular. 'Will she watch a chic flick and pamper herself?' I recalled the first time I'd seen Ellie with a thick white substance on her face and had hidden behind the sofa. This only happened when Ben was out with his friends and I prepared myself for the shock in case Gina decided to do the same.

'Steve's coming round,' said Lola.

'Ah.' The effort she'd made now made sense. Just the mention of his name could make me feel good and I felt my tail wag gently at the thought of seeing Steve-the-Cheese.

Shortly after, there was a 'Hellooeee,' followed by padding noises on the tiled floors. The humans kissed for longer than a usual welcome kiss and Obie jumped up, trying to get in between them. While he was causing a kerfuffle, Lola and I greeted Baxter and Lexi.

'How are you both?' she asked.

'I'm great, thanks, Lola,' said Lexi, her soprano tones perfectly matching the way she looked. 'Baxter's getting there but we're not quite over it yet, are we my friend?'

'I've had better times.' Baxter said in his deep, rich, voice, 'but I'm trying to stay positive.'

Not for the first time it struck me that they made an unusual pair. Massive Baxter with his posh voice and anxiety issues, and little Lexi who, one would imagine, would be the most anxious of them both due to her size, but wasn't. He seemed to be happy to go along with whatever she said and she was more concerned about his welfare than her own. He sounded so refined that I wondered if he and Lola had had a similar start in life. If so, what had gone wrong for him to end up in a rescue centre? Life could change so quickly I thought, and a memory of being thrown off a boat briefly came to mind. I shook my head to rid myself of the image. I had no plans to ask Baxter about his past; he was anxious enough as it was and I didn't want to add to his problems.

'Do you still have issues being on your own?' I asked instead, knowing he was even more afraid when he couldn't see Lexi. Lola told me not to be so nosey.

'It's all right, Lola. It helps to talk.'

Our conversation stopped there as Steve and Gina broke from their embrace. Steve said hello, which got our attention. Or it could have been that he produced a paper bag and showed us some cheese.

'You're going to make them fat, Steve.'

'Don't worry, they'll be fine when I get them on the exercise programme next week. A little cheese today won't do any harm.'

Exercise programme. What exercise programme? I looked at Lola and she appeared as confused as I was.

'Lots of exercise and less food,' said Baxter.

'How are they?' Gina nodded towards Baxter and Lexi and we listened as they talked.

'Lexi was lucky that Baxter's body shielded her from the fire. She still gets a little breathless from the smoke inhalation but is getting better each day. Baxter's on the mend; but his neck and the areas surrounding it are still very tender, that's why he wears his cravat.'

'I do think he likes it though,' said Gina, 'and it kind of suits him.'

'There you go again, putting human emotions on animals. He's a dog, Gina and he couldn't care less.'

They looked over at us and we all stared, trying to convey the fact that we *could* care less. Gina and Steve laughed.

'Perhaps you're right,' he said as he leaned into her and stroked his hand down her cheek.

'You know very well I'm right. You just have to...'

Steve-the-Cheese silenced her next words with a long kiss and we looked away to give them some privacy.

'What were you saying,' he asked when they came up for air.

'I think the trauma of the fire will take longer to get over than any physical injuries,' Gina said, her face turning serious.

'You're right. But they seem to be coping well. As long as they're together. Baxter was tired yesterday so I went to take Lexi to the garden while he was sleeping. He woke up and howled. She was by his side in a second and calmed him down. It was amazing to watch. I was going to keep Baxter and put Lexi up for adoption but now I know they'll both be with me for life.'

'You're great with them, Steve and that'll make their lives easier,' she hesitated and chewed her bottom lip.

'What is it Gina?'

'Have you seen your near neighbours yet? Do they know you're living in the village? It can't be easy for you, Steve, and I worry about you and the dogs. You know how dangerous those men are...'

'They are dangerous. But if I sat back and did nothing after what's happened to me, what sort of man would that make me? Certainly not one worthy of your attention.'

Gina blushed and I was impressed with Steve's diversionary tactics.

'She's not that dumb,' said Lola. 'But I do believe she's in love so we'll see how much of his flattery she believes.'

If I was right about his body language, I believed that Steve was as besotted with Gina as she was with him.

'...But to answer your question,' Steve continued, 'I have seen them, but only briefly when I was out walking the dogs yesterday, so they now know I live in the village. Baxter's nose alerted me to their presence before I saw them.'

Gina raised her eyebrows in question.

'He howled and started shaking. Lexi cried out too but only once. Then two men came around the corner towards me. They stared and smirked as they walked past and it reminded me of school playground bullies.'

Baxter whimpered. Lexi leaned up and nuzzled his ear before curling into him. Gina left the sofa and sat on the floor next to them.

'It's okay, boy. You're safe here with us. You both are.'

Baxter snuggled into her and whimpered again, a softer sound this time. I knew he felt better and was trying it on to get more cuddles but I would have done the same in his situation. Knowing she wouldn't get the same attention from Gina, Lexi approached Steve who picked her up, cuddling her into his body. She gave a contented sigh and I watched as she closed her eyes in ecstasy.

The worry for me was that I knew Gina was lying. I could tell by her body language and the faint, different odour she gave off when she told Baxter he was safe. I'd smelt this before when she'd been talking to the kids and had kept some truths from them, in order to protect them. When she was satisfied Baxter was calm, Gina returned to the sofa. Steve put Lexi down next to Baxter and caressed the back of Gina's hand as they talked.

'The twins and their gang must also know that I'm building a new rescue centre on the edge of the village.'

'Well that's all we need, another building going up in smoke!' said Gina. The mood seemed to be broken as she pulled her hand away from Steve's, folded her arms around her stomach and leaned forward.

'If they've done their homework, they will know I have twenty-four-hour security on site. And trust me, Gina, I don't plan on putting any dogs in there until it's one hundred per cent safe and secure.'

Baxter sighed and they both laughed, lightening the mood a little.

'What about them?' Gina nodded to Baxter.

'The big fellow has grown on me and so has Lexi. They're staying with me wherever I live.' He gave Gina a pointed look and their eyes locked.

'What can we do about the twins?' she asked, changing the subject.

'You can't do anything, Gina, it's too dangerous...'

'I've managed very well on my own up to now, thank you very much,' she interrupted.

'I know that. But now that I'm here I want to look after you and you have to admit those guys are pretty dangerous.'

'So you really think they started the fire at your centre?'

'I had my suspicions, Gina, but when I saw the way Baxter and Lexi reacted when they smelt them, everything made sense and I'm absolutely convinced. It's more than just gut instinct. I just have to work out a way to catch them.'

'What's your plan?'

'I'll let you know as soon as I have one. Shall we watch the movie?'

They headed for the kitchen to get some drinks and chocolate before settling down to watch the film. While they were out of the room, Lola looked pointedly at Baxter and Lexi.

'So you knew about the twins. Why didn't you tell us you'd seen them?'

'Steve takes us everywhere,' said Lexi, 'and we've heard him talk about what they've done. I know how frightening it must have been for you all, Lola, so we didn't want to raise the subject and risk upsetting you.'

'We agreed the best course of action was to keep quiet,' Baxter added.

How thoughtful that the newbies had considered our feelings, despite what they'd been through. The more I got to know this big, soft dog, and the little fluffy one, the more I liked them.

'How very decent of you,' said Lola, and I could see she was trying not to get emotional. She harrumphed, then returned to her business-like self. 'We need to get together next week to discuss our options. We must do everything we can to help Steve.'

Baxter lifted his head and the fear in his eyes was palpable. Lexi licked him again and snuggled into him, comforting and reassuring.

'Not you, old boy,' Lola said. 'We will need you and Lexi to stay with Steve as much as you can, so you can report back anything you might think is of value to us. Do you think you can manage that?'

'We're traumatised,' Baxter responded, speaking for them both, 'not completely stupid.' Lexi rolled onto her back, her tail wagging furiously while Baxter smirked. Lola had the grace to look embarrassed. 'I'll try to concentrate and give you any information that you need.'

'Me too,' said Lexi.

'Obie?' asked Lola.

'Do I have a choice?' he asked, and we all laughed quietly.

If only we had known then what the following week had in store; none of us would be laughing for a long time.

Chapter 5

It was Tuesday evening. I only knew this because Ellie and I were settling down in front of the screen in the living room so she could watch what Ben called her favourite programme, which was set in a hospital. From their discussions, I knew this was where people went to be cured if they were sick, or even to die if they were coming to the end of their lives. It was like the vets, but for people. I made my own assumption that people liked watching drama in others' lives to make them feel better about their own lives. Ben, who was about to attend a quiz night with his friends, confirmed my assumption when I'd heard him say, 'Soaps were invented by governments to make miserable people feel happier about their lot.'

Just as Ben was about to leave, Ellie's phone rang.

'See you two later,' he mouthed, before kissing her on the head and giving me a pat. I would have preferred to have gone to the quiz night in the tavern but knew Ellie would stop there on our final walk of the day when we'd say hello to everyone and Ben would accompany us home.

'What?' she said into her phone. 'Again? I don't believe it, Gina. This can't be happening. Stay where you are. I'll get Ben and we'll be there as soon as we can.' Her voice had risen to a screech so I knew something awful had happened. She rushed outside with me close on her heels.

'Ben, Ben,' she shouted as she approached the gate, but Ben had disappeared around the corner and didn't hear her. 'Damn,' said Ellie looking down at her bare feet. I ran back into the house and carefully picked up her phone, then trotted down the path to the gate with it in my mouth.

'Of course! I'm glad one of us has a brain, Sandy,' she said.

Ellie held the phone to her ear. 'Ben, Obie's missing again. Can you come home now, please, and I'll explain more. No, he hasn't just run away again, come home, please...'

Less than a minute later, Ben appeared. We all went into the house and Ellie ran upstairs to get her outside shoes and clothes. She returned almost naked, and dressed as she talked.

'So Gina phoned...'

'I know that,' Ben interrupted. 'But what makes her think Obie was taken, rather than he's just done his usual and run away again?'

'As I was saying, Gina phoned and said she saw Obie being bundled into the back of a van.'

'What the hell?'

'Exactly. She was on her way home and had just turned left onto her street and noticed the open van outside her house. As she neared it, a man wearing a balaclava ran out of her open gate carrying Obie. Can you imagine how frightening that must have been?'

So Obie had been dognapped yet again. I knew he would be terrified and hoped it wasn't too late for us to save him.

We rushed to Gina's. On arrival outside, we noticed one of her car's front tyres was flat and wondered if that was anything to do with what had happened earlier. Steve-the-Cheese was already inside. He was sitting on the floor beside Baxter who was very agitated. As could only be expected, Gina was distraught and her face was a mass of worry. Laura was sitting on the sofa cuddling Lexi and crying.

'Greg?' asked Ellie.

'He's in his room. Lola's with him so I know she'll be comforting him. But poor Lola is distressed too. She's got a small mark on her face so I guess one of them must have hit her. I'll need to take her to the vet after the police have left. They're on their way now.'

How awful, I thought. I had an urgent desire to see Lola as soon as I could but knew she'd want me to listen to our people, to discover if they had any plans and where we would fit in. I also knew she'd be putting on a brave face to give Greg the impression the worst was over and also to give him as much comfort as she could. Like me, she would be terrified for Obie.

'Are you okay?' Ben asked Gina. 'I know it's a stupid question but it must have been terrifying.'

'Laura, go to your room.'

'I'm going to be sixteen this year, Mum. I'm old enough to know what's going on and I need to know what happened, even if it was scary.'

I saw the look of resignation and understanding on Gina's face. 'Don't blame me if you get nightmares, Laura.'

'I'm not five years old, Mum.'

That got a smile from everyone and released some of the tension.

'You already know that as I approached our house I saw a man in a balaclava coming out of the gate with Obie in his arms. Obie was yelping and struggling - he must have been terrified!' Gina let out a sob and Steve left Baxter and moved to her side. He put an arm around her and she leant into him.

'You don't have to do this if it upsets you.'

Gina gave Steve a weak smile. 'I want to get it out now so that I'll be able to tell the police without being too emotional.' She kissed him on the lips and they looked into each other's eyes. It was an intensely private moment, as if they'd forgotten we were there.

'Hello. Remember us?' said Laura, and Gina looked embarrassed for a second. Laura was growing up fast and sometimes it was like she was the mother and Gina the teenager.

'The man had a firm hold of Obie. As I slammed my foot on the brakes and came to a sudden halt, it was as if my world turned to slow motion. One of the back doors of their van was open and he rushed towards it and flung Obie in the back as if he was a bag of rubbish – there were other dogs in there and they were all yelping. I was terrified but furious too, so I jumped out of the car and ran towards the van which was just pulling off and turning around. I rushed back to my car, put it in reverse and tried to follow. Even though I was panicking, I thought I could call Steve or the police while I followed. Anyway, as they came almost level with my car, the one in the passenger seat picked up a shot gun.'

'Oh, no!' said Ellie, shaking her head in horror. 'No, no, no.'

Laura had one hand over her open mouth by this stage and held Lexi with the other. Ellie moved to sit on the arm of her chair. Putting an arm around her, she gave her a squeeze.

'I'm all right,' she said. 'It's just that it's so shocking. These things happen to other people; you don't expect them to happen to your own family.'

'Did he hurt you, Mum? Are you going to be all right?'

'I'm fine, Laura. He didn't hurt me.'

She clearly wasn't fine.

As I looked around at the concerned faces, I could see they all knew that but it had reassured Laura for the moment, as Gina had intended. She continued.

'He fired and I waited to feel some sort of pain. When I felt nothing I tried to move the car but it felt uneven - then I realised he must have been shooting at the tyre. I grabbed my phone, got out of the car and chased the van. I took a photo but I don't know if it will be any use to the police. I stopped following it when I realised they were now shooting at me, and the van disappeared into the distance.'

'A man was shooting at you from a van and you chased it? Are you crazy!' Laura screamed at her mother. Lexi wriggled out of Laura's grasp and joined Baxter on the floor.

'I'm all right, Laura. We're all fine except for poor Obie. What do you think they'll do to him, Steve?'

They hadn't noticed that Greg was now standing by the door listening, and Lola was with him.

'Well, if they shoot at people planning to hurt them, they're not going to be bothered about looking after a dog are they? That's the last we'll see of Obie, for sure,' Laura said bluntly, then she put her head in her hands and sobbed.

'Noooooo!' Greg screamed. He gazed wildly at everyone, then ran back into his room and slammed the door.

'I'll go,' said Ben, getting up from his chair. I knew that Ben had a good rapport with Greg, so it made sense. Before Lola followed him, she nodded her head towards me, then to Gina and Steve. I got the message loud and clear. Ellie was holding Laura and speaking to her gently; but Gina and Steve were talking on the settee. I sat by their feet and listened.

'This wouldn't have happened if they had been able to take Baxter and Lexi. I'll check the security camera footage but when I went to pick up my laptop earlier, the gates were open and I always close them. I wondered if the postie or a meter reader had been there, but they've always used the gate by the footpath in the past, never the gates by the drive.'

'I don't know, Steve. But it doesn't make any difference does it? Obie's been taken again, and if the poor thing does survive this, he'll never be the same again.'

'There's more to this, Gina, as well you know.' He was holding both of her hands by this stage. 'I've brought trouble to your door and as long as they know you're part of my life, you and the kids are in danger, and so is anyone associated with you and me. I think we should stop seeing each other until I can put a stop to this business, and get those b...,' he glanced towards Laura and Ellie, '...those *scumbags* behind bars once and for all.'

'But Obie was dognapped before I even met you, Steve, and they might have found out that Ellie, Ben and I spoke to Sergeant Christo. This might have nothing to do with you at all. There were other dogs in their van too, so it's not just about us, is it?'

'Trust me, Gina. It's me they want and they'll do anything they can to get me off the island. Look at what they did to my centre and the poor dogs in there - and everyone thinks they started that fire in the forest when Ben, Ellie and Sandy were endangered. They have no morals and want revenge for the suspended sentence and the loss of face. That makes them dangerous. Very dangerous indeed.'

'Listen to me, Steve,' Gina moved her hands to Steve's cheeks so that he couldn't move his head away, even if he wanted to. 'We are in this together-unless this is an excuse to end our relationship...'

'As if, Gina,' he protested.

'Good. Because I've waited a long time for someone like you to come into my life, and I'm not going to let any criminal bullies split us up, no matter how dangerous it gets.'

'But I'm worried about you and the children, Gina. If anything happened to you guys I'd never forgive myself.'

'Well, we'll just have to come up with a plan to make sure nothing does happen, and to take these scumbags down while we're at it.'

Neither of them noticed that Ellie and Laura had stopped talking and were listening to everything they said.

'Well said, Mum,' said Laura, once her mother had finished talking. 'I quite like having Steve around too. He makes you happy and when you're happy, so are we - me and Greg, I mean.'

'Oh, Laura, come here,' Gina said, and I sighed happily as I saw mother and daughter hugging on the sofa. Ben and Greg came back into the room shortly after and Greg wormed his way in between Laura and Gina to join the family hug. Lola put her front paws onto the sofa and her head on Gina's lap and Laura stroked her. I could see that Lola wasn't in any pain now, and that was a big relief.

I returned to Ben and Ellie, wondering what plan our people would devise in an attempt to avert further danger and to stop the twins once and for all.

I also wondered if Lola had any ideas for us to save Obie from the torture he would surely suffer.

My thoughts were broken by the ringing doorbell. It was Sergeant Christo and a few other plain-clothes policemen. We said goodbye to Gina and the others for now, and she promised she would let Ben and Ellie know what the police intended to do. As Steve walked us to the door, he pulled Ben back; from what I could hear of his muttered words, he was arranging to meet him in the tavern, to discuss the way forward. I aimed to go with Ben so I could find out what Steve planned.

They were cooking a big breakfast the following day so it must still be the weekend and a work free day for them both. I was still agitated and worried about Obie and although I was salivating when I smelt the bacon cooking, I wasn't my usual enthusiastic self when I ate it – I was simply going through the motions.

'What's wrong, Sandy, are you missing Obie?' asked Ellie.

She was spot on as usual, and always picked up on my moods.

'She's a dog,' said Ben, 'and won't have a clue what's going on.'

Ben should have known me better by now so I went to lie by Ellie after breakfast. She called me up onto the settee, and stroked and cuddled me, whispering that it would be all right and they'd do everything they could to get Obie back safe and sound. I guess Ben was feeling left out because he joined us, and although he didn't say anything, he did make me feel a little better by stroking and caressing me. He was kind. *I shouldn't be so hard on him*, I told myself, just because he's less sensitive than Ellie.

A little later in the day, they started tidying up outside and preparing food in the kitchen. I assumed we were having visitors for the afternoon meal and Ben was cleaning the outside cooker so it looked like a barbecue was on the horizon. Gina and Steve-the-Cheese turned up not much later, with Lola, Baxter and Lexi in tow.

'Laura's gone to the Mall with Katie, and Greg's gone for tea with his friends so it's just us three,' Gina said. There was no spark in her eyes and I knew she was missing my pal.

Lola said as much. 'It's as if they've decided we're not getting him back, Sandy. I can't imagine the pain and indignities he's going through, the poor, poor boy.'

Thanks for making me feel even worse, Lola. 'It is beyond belief that they would target him yet again. Obie must feel like the whole world is against him, if he's still with us.'

'Don't ever say that, Sandy!' Lola raised her voice and our people parents stopped talking and looked towards us.

'Sandy was probably a bit too rough,' said Steve, as Lola and I nuzzled each other. Baxter and Lexi listened to our conversation but hadn't said anything, until now.

'Steve thinks they came for us but took Obie and the other dogs when they couldn't get us,' said Lexi. 'He's trying to find out what other dogs are missing from the village and who they belong to.'

'That means we're still not safe, and never will be,' said Baxter. It was too much for the big fellow and he started howling.

'Oh no, not again.' Steve rushed to him. 'It'll be all right, pal. I'll look after you. Okay, it's okay.' The soothing words and the gentle stroking calmed Baxter who lay down and closed his eyes. As usual, Lexi curled up next to him. Her reassuring presence always seemed to lessen his anxiety and he was asleep within a few minutes.

'What are we going to do about Baxter and Lexi?' I asked Lola out of their earshot.

'I was going to avail their services for Intelligence purposes, the same as Tulip, to inform us about the twins' comings and goings, but it looks like they'll be with Steve twenty-four, seven,' Lola replied. 'So we will treat Baxter with gentle care and help him to rebuild confidence in people. I'm not sure about Lexi, she hides her feelings, but maybe her way of coping is looking after Baxter. We'll keep an eye on her, just in case it becomes too much.'

'Sounds like a good plan,' I said.

'Yes indeed. And we'll do exactly the same with Obie when he comes home.'

'So you believe he is going to come home?'

'We'll get him back, old girl, one way or another. Anything else doesn't bear thinking about. Now, let's listen to what our people have to say about the situation.'

I tried to put the terrifying thoughts of Obie out of my head as we settled down to eavesdrop on our families.'

They chit-chatted for a while, trying to pretend that life was normal and enjoying the moment, but it was obvious to me they were putting off the inevitable and I wondered when they would have the important discussions.

It happened after they ate.

'They're showing the match in the tavern,' said Ben. 'Fancy it, Steve?'

There was no protest from the women as the men started to get ready. Lola nodded at me discreetly, which I assumed meant she wanted me to go with the men. It didn't occur to me to argue the toss so, as Steve went to the utility room to get the harness for Baxter and lead for Lexi, I got up, stretched and walked towards Ben with my tail wagging in expectation.

'Aw, Sandy wants to go with you, Ben.'

'It'll be too much with Sandy, Baxter, and Lexi, Ellie, especially if there's a big crowd and the blokes start getting excited.'

Charming.

Gina looked at me, then at Steve, then back to me. I acted as if I hadn't seen anything but sat down by Ben and pawed him gently. In case he didn't get the message I gave him my most soulful eyes look.

'She is just so damn gorgeous,' Ellie said, jumping up and tickling me first under the chin, then behind the ears. I noticed the other dogs raising their eyebrows, trying to hide their smiles.

'Actually, Ben,' said Steve. 'Sandy gets along well with Baxter and Lexi, so perhaps she should come with us.'

I never doubted it for a minute. I did a celebratory little twirl, then waited while Ben went to fetch my lead.

'I think she's got that twirl thing from Chip,' said Ellie, 'and picking up pinecones to play with. It's hilarious to watch.'

'Clever, Sandy,' said Gina, and then she decided to cuddle and kiss me, too. I was more than happy with the reactions from our people and delighted that their training was progressing so well.

A little nudge from Lola reminded me that I had work to do.

'Remember to listen to every word,' she said. 'You're Fish for the next few hours, not Sandy. This is your mission, old girl, and I want you to pay attention and remain alert. Help Lexi to keep an eye on the big fellow too.' She whispered the latter so the others wouldn't hear.

Shortly after, we were all geared up and it was time to hit the road. The men were quiet so I walked in front when Ben extended my lead. I was careful to stay within earshot, just in case they decided to chat. Baxter and Lexi initially walked by Steve's side, but we were all surprised when the big dog lengthened his gait and caught up with me. Lexi's little legs were going nineteen to the dozen and she caught up eventually.

'Hello, there,' I said, acting as if this was his usual behaviour.

'I'm trying my best, Sandy,' he said. 'Small steps at a time.'

Good on him. I knew how hard he found some activities that came as second nature to me and many other dogs, not just squad members. Lexi wasn't on the full extension of her lead and was able to run further ahead, assuming that Baxter wanted a private word with me.

I noticed a cat staring from under a car on the other side of the road. I recognised it as the tom that had a head too large for its body that I'd seen on previous walks, and knew it was trouble; I'd had to warn it off a few times already. If push came to shove, I wouldn't like to get into a scrap with it as it looked vicious and acted very streetwise. It oozed out from under the car and sauntered towards Lexi who was busy sniffing a bush that had recently been scented, and I wasn't sure she'd seen him. I knew Baxter had seen the feline and expected him to back off, or to hide behind Steve like the wuss he was-very unkind of me I know, but it was my honest opinion.

The cat hissed and walked faster, heading directly towards our fluffy Maltese pal. Lexi looked up as the cat, almost twice her size, swiped a paw towards her. She managed to jump back out of the way in the nick of time.

'I'm sick of everyone thinking they can have a go,' Baxter growled. He leapt at the cat who had to do a pretty nifty roll to avoid Baxter's massive paws. Steve was using all of his strength to pull his dog back.

'Good boy, Baxter! That showed it who's boss. Come on now, back to me.'

Lexi didn't seem too bothered and barked a thank you. The cat fled back under the car from where he hissed and screeched as we passed. I'm sure Baxter held his head higher as he trotted towards Steve and was rewarded with a few pats. I was gobsmacked by his reaction, and immensely proud of the big dog who hadn't thought twice about helping his friend who was in danger. I couldn't wait to tell Lola later. Baxter was making an effort to overcome his fears and anxieties and what a way to start!

We arrived at the tavern a few minutes later. I headed for our usual area which housed the big TV, between the inside and outside of the tavern but was surprised when Ben tugged my lead and we followed Steve to a quiet table outside.

Our hosts brought beers for the men and bowls of water for us and the two men got down to business straight away.

'You know I need to visit their base and...'

'*We* need to, Steve. We're all at risk here and I'm not letting you do this on your own.'

'So you're in then?'

'Most definitely.'

'So, we must make a visit to the other end of the island. It's no secret that their business is there but I'm not sure exactly where. Panni has contacts and is going to help with that.'

'Who's Panni?'

'He works for me but we grew up together here and in the UK. I'd trust him with my life.'

'He's not worried about putting himself or his family in danger?'

'He's as upset about the fire and the dogs as I am. He also knows how to be discreet, Ben, and all I'm going to say is that he has various talents that will be a bonus for this sort of work. People don't mess with Panni.'

Panni sounded interesting. I made a mental note to ask Baxter if he knew anything about him.

'I don't want the women or children to have any involvement in this,' Ben said. He took before a large swig of his amber liquid. 'Ellie has to go to the UK shortly for some legal business she can't do from over here, so from my point of view, that's the best time for us to sort out this pond life, once and for all.'

'I'm hoping to convince Gina to go away too, with Laura and Greg. I know her mother's ill and she wants to take the kids to see her.'

'Don't you want to meet her family?'

'Not yet, Ben. It would only confuse her mother - she has dementia. This is the real thing for me and Gina and I won't let anyone or anything spoil it. I want to protect her and the best way to do that is to sort out the twins and their cronies.'

'You know it's not going to be easy don't you? Ellie wants me to leave it to the police, and from what she says, Gina wants the same.'

'And in an ideal world that would happen. Sergeant Christo is great, but I've heard his immediate superior is in cahoots with the twins, and the PC who was with him when we first met seems really dodgy to me.'

'Absolutely. It was obvious he knew at least one of them and was keen to help them. So, we agree that we need to try to get Ellie and Gina to go away at the same time, then we act while they're away?'

Steve nodded.

'We'll have less than a month in my estimation; but in the meantime, you'll ask Panni to find out more so then we can come up with some sort of plan? Is that about right, Steve?'

'Spot on, Ben. This is going to be dangerous and I'm not exaggerating when I say our lives will be at risk. Are you sure you want to be involved?'

'I'm already involved and I'll do whatever it takes to ensure the safety and wellbeing of my family. If anything happened to Ellie or Sandy...'

I noticed he hadn't mentioned Mia and wondered whether she would ever return to the island. I swallowed a lump in my throat as I watched Ben trying to hide his emotions. The men I knew were very different to the women-instead of letting it all go, they did their best to fight any strong emotions, in public anyway.

I was determined that we would accompany Ben and Steve on their mission and hoped Lola felt the same. I would go without her if necessary but didn't believe it would come to that. Whatever happened, our people were going to need all the help they could get.

When their serious conversation ended they decided to move into the TV Room. The whistle went for half-time just as we entered and some of the men inside called hello to Ben and Steve.

'Nice dog,' said one as he stumbled towards me and I swiftly side-stepped to avoid him. He stank of the liquid Ben enjoyed and his eyes were struggling to focus.

'Aw, don't be like that,' he said, either ignoring, or being unable to read my body language.

'Leave her, Mal,' said Ben. Out of nowhere, Mal attempted to throw a punch at him. 'You telegraphed that one, my friend,' said Ben, as he caught onto Mal's wrist and held it in a vice-like grip, not acting as if he was his friend.

Baxter, who had been doing his best to ignore the kerfuffle, suddenly stood up to his full height and growled. 'Don't you dare threaten my pack. Now go away, you horrid, despicable, man.'

'Go, Baxter,' said Lexi, egging him on.

'Okay, okay, I was just trying to be friendly like. Call off the beast and I'll be on my way. No hard feelings, eh.'

As he staggered out of the building, the men at the tables he bumped into called out to him, telling him he should learn to hold his drink and that it was time to go home. He seemed unaware of the abuse and it was quiet after he left until one of the others spoke.

'Is that big dog dangerous, Steve?'

'Only if you threaten one of us with violence. Come on over and say hello.'

'You sure?'

I struggled to believe anyone could be afraid of Baxter, but then again, all they had seen was a big dog who had just put a grown man in his place. They didn't know the big beastie was a walking mass of anxiety.

'Aw, you frightened of the big dopey-looking dog?' asked one of the man's friends, and if he didn't want anyone else taking the mickey, the man who'd asked about Baxter knew he'd now have to come and say hello and stroke the dog. He was tentative but Baxter made it easy when he rolled onto his back and let the man tickle his belly. I had no idea what had happened to him tonight but he acted like he'd had a personality transplant.

'He's just a big softy,' said the man, and not for the first time I wondered how some men could act so macho with each other, but turn to mush when they started petting us dogs. If only all of them were like this, there'd be no need for rescue centres.

A couple of others came to say hello and Lexi was so cute that she also got lots of attention. Fed up with being ignored, I did a few twirls and gave my best *come and stroke me* look. Obviously it worked and I got the attention I knew I deserved until someone shouted that the second half was about to start, when everyone returned to their seats. Baxter, Lexi, and I lay down to watch some men run around a field chasing a ball. It reminded me of some of the dogs I'd met in the rescue centre where I used to live. They didn't want my ball until I was playing with it, then they would chase me for it, some of them getting quite aggressive.

The match finished with Ben's team winning and Steve's coming a poor second.

'Losers, losers,' Ben chanted a few times on the walk home. Steve refused to rise to the bait so Ben eventually moved on and chatted about the rules of the game and who would be picked for the team next time. I wondered if they were going to talk to Ellie and Gina about visiting the home country tonight, or whether that would wait until another day.

As it happened, Ellie and Gina had their own plans.

Ben's phone bleeped during the short walk home and he fished it out of his pocket. Steve waited patiently to hear if he was going to share the news, and so did we three.

'Ellie said there've been developments at home. It's about our niece, Mia, but I've no idea what.' He was still looking at his phone as he talked, and tapping away at it with his clunky fingers.

'Whoa!' Steve shouted a warning and dragged Ben away from the lamppost he was about to walk into.

'Thanks, Buddy,' Ben said, putting his phone back in his pocket. 'This can wait.'

We rounded the corner heading for home. A stone had been placed on the pillar next to the gate. Ben shrugged his shoulders and lifted it. There was something underneath and I heard ripping and watched as Ben paused again, looking at a piece of paper that had been lodged there.

'Oh no.' He rubbed a hand through his hair and handed the paper to Steve.

'It's got to be those damned twins. We can't tell the women about this, they're frightened enough as it is.'

'Too right,' Ben replied. 'But it's even more important that we get them both away to safety as soon as possible. Let me destroy that before either of them see it.'

'No way. I'm giving this to Sergeant Christo and I'm going to ask him if he's found out about the other dogs that were taken. I'm more convinced by the minute that the twins are getting wary-they're like rats backing into a corner,' Steve said as he put the paper into the inside pocket of his jacket.

'And you know what happens when rats are backed into a corner?'

'They go for your throat. That's a pleasant thought to greet the women with. We need to try to act as if nothing's happened, come on.'

Well, that's a lovely way to end the evening, I thought as we walked up the path to the house. The men took a deep breath before unlocking the door and walking in.

The TV was off and there were two empty glasses on the coffee table. Ellie's eyes looked red and Gina also seemed sad. Lola lay on the sofa next to Gina who was stroking her absentmindedly. The women were too distracted to pick up on the tension displayed by the men, which seemed obvious to me. It was also obvious to Lola who jumped off the sofa and headed for the kitchen. I followed and lapped at the water from my bowl. She raised an eyebrow and, as quickly as I could, I explained what I thought had been found under the stone.

'Before they found it they'd already decided that Gina, the kids, and Ellie should take a trip off the island. Now they know we're all in danger so it's doubly urgent.'

'I wondered why they were so uptight,' she whispered back. 'But it's worked out well, Fish old girl. Ellie's sister has been misbehaving again. Ellie said she needs to see Mia and to sort everything out, whether the courts agree or not.'

'I wonder what she means by sorting everything out?'

Steve came into the utility room just then, followed by Baxter and Lexi. He opened a few cupboards before Ben called to him. 'The cupboard on the left above the sink, mate.'

Taking out a bowl, Steve filled it with water and put it in front of his dogs. He patted them, then scratched me behind an ear and gave Lola a belly rub. If there's one thing you could say about Steve-the-Cheese, he was pretty generous with his affection, and very fair. We waited for him to leave the room before continuing.

'Both Gina and Ellie are going away,' Baxter said. 'They're talking about it now, that's what we came in here to tell you.'

'And that's what I was going to tell Sandy, old chap. Gina's mother is poorly and will have difficulty recognising Laura and Greg if they leave it much longer apparently. So they'll be in the same country and will be able to support each other. But Gina's also worried about Obie and is trying to hide it-but aren't we all...?'

We all thought about Obie for a moment, and I hate to admit it, but I did wonder if he was still alive. An involuntary cry escaped me and Ellie came running into the room.

'Oh, poor baby,' she said as she bent down to my level and put her arms around me. 'You can pick up on all our worries can't you? Will a little treat make you feel better?'

Lola rolled her eyes as Ellie went to the treat cupboard and picked out a little bone-shaped biscuit. Then she looked at my companions and got out another three. It was a good antidote for the worry about Obie, and there were soon four busy tails competing for space in the small room.

'Come on you lot,' said Ellie and we followed her into the living room.

We still paid attention to the conversation as we chewed on the delicious treats.

'I know you'll have to take time off work, Ben and it's a worry about the house. But it's Sandy I'm worried about more than anyone else. Who can we leave her with that we can trust one hundred percent?'

'Ordinarily, I would say me,' said Steve, 'but if I'm looking after Baxter, Lexi, and Lola, and sorting out the new centre and the safety of the animals there, I'm not sure I'll have the time. Sorry guys but I'm just...'

'Not a problem at all,' said Ben. 'We fully understand. Ellie, under the circumstances I think I should stay put to look after Sandy and the house. We've also got a big project going on in work and the boss needs me. I'll come if you insist - but you're going to have enough on your plate without having to worry whether Sandy and the house are safe.'

'So I'll have you, Sandy, *and* the house to worry about instead, Ben. How's that going to work?'

'But who knows what might happen to the house or Sandy if we're both away,' asked Ben, 'And what about your place, Gina? It could be a target if it's empty.'

Nice deflection Ben, I thought.

'I've only a small number of valuables at my place,' said Steve. 'I can take them to Gina's and can stay there with my dogs and Lola. If you think that will work?' he added the last after Gina seemed to be pondering the idea.

'But I wouldn't want to inconvenience...'

'It's not a problem. Mine's a new rental and my own furniture is still in storage, so it makes sense to move to yours. I spend loads of time there already and some of my stuff is there.'

We all watched Gina blush like a young girl, and Lola suppressed a chuckle.

'Ben?'

'You know I'd rather be with you, Ellie. But...'

'I know that, love, and I will worry about you and Sandy. If you think it's too dangerous we should all just get the hell out of Dodge.'

They all laughed at her words before things turned serious again. 'I'm pretty sure we'll be safe here and you can both do what you have to do without worrying about us.'

'Of course,' Ellie and Gina said in unison.

I looked at all of our people and wondered why none of them wanted to tell the truth. Recalling various events throughout my life, I knew no good could come of lies. The truth always came out in the end.

Chapter 6

It seemed to me that Ellie and Gina had been away for ages. Though we weren't aware of anything happening, Ben was tense and upset when we met up with the others for a walk on Saturday morning. I could sense that Steve-the-Cheese was tense too; Lola confirmed this.

'I've had another note,' we heard Ben tell Steve. 'Left this morning, telling me they know where Ellie is. Can you believe it?' He rubbed his hand through his hair.

'You know they're bluffing, Ben. There's no way they could know. Sergeant Christo knows of at least two other dog owners who've had notes, and he suspects there are more, with ransom demands too.'

'That's terrible and you're probably right about them bluffing, but there's that bit of doubt niggling away at me. This is one of the few occasions I'm glad Ellie's going on a shopping trip with Gina, and overnighting in the airport hotel before the flight. There's no way they'll know about that, unless they've got hold of the flight manifest of course...'

He let the words hang in the air and Steve let out an incredulous laugh. 'Listen to yourself, Ben. There's no way these guys can get access to that sort of information. Look man,' they stopped walking as Steve put a hand on

Ben's arm. 'It's worrying that anyone would do this, I know. But they're playing with your mind. Ellie and Gina are perfectly safe.'

'You're right, they are playing with my head, and it's having the result they probably wanted. We have to stop this once and for all.'

'I agree. Everything's set up for tomorrow. We'll be all done before Gina and the kids and Ellie return. Are you sure you're up for this?'

'Of course.' Ben shook Steve's hand off his arm. 'Are you?'

'One hundred per cent.'

They carried on walking. Ben let me off the lead and Lola nodded that I should jog ahead with Baxter and Lexi. When she caught us up she whispered. 'Act as if nothing is going on. Sandy, get to Chip as soon as you can. We're going to need him with us tomorrow.

I gave a gentle bark in agreement, then ran ahead to discover some new and interesting smells in the bondu, hoping they would temporarily take my mind off the mission of the following day.

There weren't any opportunities to sneak out of the house during the day. Ben was tense one moment and hyper the next and I had more walks that Saturday than was usual. Not that I complained. He watched TV for most of the night, and after his video call with Ellie, drank lots of the amber liquid he always enjoyed. He'd nodded off on the sofa, and though I would normally have loved this and cuddled into him for the night, it didn't suit my plans for tonight. I pretended to have a bad dream and waggled my paws for a bit. No response from Ben, so I cried out. Still nothing, so I had to bark a few times before he woke. He must have been in a deep sleep because he sat bolt upright, and when I took a peek, I realised it was taking him a moment to come to.

'What is it, Sandy, is someone there?' Ben asked before seeing my moving paws and mouth. I gave a little cry and he cottoned on.

'Come on, it's only a bad dream,' he said, stroking me gently.

I felt a little guilty for waking him so suddenly, knowing he would think there were intruders. But it was a means to an end, and now that Ben knew there was nothing majorly untoward, he relaxed.

'Let's go to bed, Sandy, and get a good night's sleep. We've both got a busy, and maybe dangerous, day tomorrow. Night night.' He gave me a final belly rub before stretching, yawning and heading up the stairs. At least now I knew I was going with him and that would make my job easier.

I went back to sleep and when I woke later it was still dark and quiet. The moon was shining through the curtains at the window and I knew it would be some time before Ben stirred. Sneaking out of the house while Ben was in bed wasn't something I wanted to do, but I had no choice. I had no idea how I was supposed to get Chip – scratch that, I had to get into mission mode, I reminded myself – get *Aden* out of his house ready to join us all first thing in the morning. That was my first task, so I had to go to him now, while nobody was about.

His house was understandably dark as I approached it. I noticed that Nicole and Mike's car was missing from the driveway, so I leapt up onto the short wall and over the other side and had a walk around, sniffing as I went. Then I positioned myself so I could look through the small gap in the curtains covering the patio door. As I had already suspected, Aden's bed wasn't there, and from what I could see, he wasn't in the room. So his people parents must be away and Aden was with someone else. But who? Then it came to me. I remembered him telling me he had slept at a different house once when Nicole and Mike had gone away on holiday. They were friends and neighbours of his people parents. He hadn't been happy, as the new people had a cat that pretended to be friendly when the people were there but wound him up when they were out. It didn't take much to wind him up so none of us had got into a conversation with him about it. I jumped over the wall into the garden next door and sniffed the air. All I could smell was the faint odour of cat - but that wasn't unusual as they passed through many gardens on their night travels. I took a moment to decide whether to keep checking this way or to change direction. I climbed onto the back wall, scaled the small fence and jumped from it directly onto the ground at the back of the houses which all backed onto the countryside. Even though I was sure no people had seen me, I wanted it to stay that way, so although there weren't any two-legged creatures about, I erred on the side of caution.

Two houses further along, I struck lucky. This one had a wall but no back fence, and when I got onto the wall I noticed a cat at the patio door. The curtains were open and I could see Aden on the inside, pacing up and down. When the cat placed a paw on the glass door and moved it around, Aden followed its every move. The cat turned to look at me. It hissed. *Friendly chap,* I thought, as I entered the garden. It hissed again and arched the middle of its back, making its intentions perfectly clear.

'Morning,' I said casually as I trotted to the door.

It must have expected a standoff, or for me to attack, and the look on its face was priceless. The cat relaxed a little but its look was still one of mistrust. At least it hadn't launched himself at me, so I did my best to ignore it and gave the door a quick once over.

'You won't get in there.'

It was my turn to be surprised as I realised the cat spoke dog.

'Thanks,' I said. 'Any suggestions?'

Relaxed in my company now, it sat down and licked a paw. I tried to be patient, knowing that cats only did what they wanted, when they wanted to, and then only when it suited them. It was probably trying to provoke a reaction from me but I decided to play its game; I lay down on the patio, folded a paw underneath me and gave a long yawn. *I have all the time in the world pussycat,* I hoped to convey, even though I was in somewhat of a hurry.

It gave a little chuckle and I was beginning to like this one, despite myself.

'They're paranoid about their house and belongings. Their dog's been stolen and you're lucky you were able to get over the wall. They're getting a new fence built next week and having some cameras put up too. There's no way you can get in or Chip can get out without waking them. Why are you here and what's going on?'

'I need some help from Ade..., Chip, tomorrow and have to get him out tonight.'

'What sort of help? Where are you going? What's happening?'

The cat was beginning to sound like Chip, though his speech was slower and more considered. I knew most cats were naturally curious and many were quite savvy, so I didn't see the point of lying. Anyway, I didn't have the time to come up with some convoluted story.

'There's some bad people on another part of the island. My people parent and a friend of his have received threats from them and are hoping to do something tomorrow to sort them out. It could well be the people who have carried out the dog-nappings. It's going to be very dangerous so they're going to need help.'

'And you want his help?' The cat nodded towards Aden who was now sitting on the other side of the patio door, tail wagging, looking from one to the other of us.

'That's right, yeah.'

'Hmm. Okay, here's my idea.'

I heard the cat out, and knowing I couldn't come up with anything better, decided to go for it. Aden had heard our conversation and as soon as I had knocked over a few of the potted plants and disappeared over the back wall, he started barking.

It didn't take long for the lights to come on and I watched as two people appeared. The man held what looked like a metal rod that had a curved thicker part at the end of it and the woman held a heavy looking ornament.

'What did you hear, boy?' I heard the woman say as the man opened the patio door.

Aden continued to bark and the lights came on upstairs in the house next door, but nobody else appeared.

As soon as the door was opened wide enough, Aden ran outside, still barking, and leapt over the wall. He continued barking for a while as he headed into the countryside, giving the impression he was chasing someone or something. I sidled along the wall and the cat called out, 'Good luck!,' as I disappeared into the countryside. I felt a little guilty, as I knew Aden's temporary people parents would worry that something had happened to him, but if all went to plan, he would be back safe and sound the following day. I didn't allow myself to think about what might happen if whatever Ben and Steve-the-Cheese had planned, failed to work.

Phase one of the extraction plan was now complete. Phase two meant working out how to get Aden into the vehicle without Ben or Steve discovering him until it was too late to turn back. Aden was all fired up which made it impossible to think clearly.

'Wherewegoing? What'shappening,Sandy? Will Ibeintrouble?'

'Get into mission mode, Aden, we leave in the morning with Bunty, Baxter, Lexi, my Ben and Steve-the-Cheese.'

'Cheese? Hmm,lovely.'

Aden could be very easily distracted and I gave him a look, which made him refocus.

'Never mind the cheese. We have to think of a way to get you into the vehicle without being seen by the men. But first, let's get some sleep and we can do that when the time comes. We'll go back to my place and you can sleep under the bar where Ben won't see you. I'll call you in for some food in the morning when Ben's in the shower.' I spoke confidently, though I didn't feel particularly certain that we wouldn't be discovered. It seemed to satisfy Aden and I heard his gentle breathing before I quietly entered the house and listened. So far, so good. All was quiet, which meant Ben was still asleep upstairs.

Chapter 7

Despite the excitement of helping Aden out of the house and the pre-mission anxiety, I managed to get some sleep. I woke to the sound of Ben moving about upstairs and gave him the usual greeting at the bottom of the stairs – the tiles on the landing were too cold to sleep on in the autumn, so I was now back in the living room, in my cosy basket with a blanket. I acted as if I hadn't seen him for weeks, knowing that he loved that.

'Morning, Sandy, lovely to see you too,' he said. 'No walk first thing this morning coz we're going to see Steve shortly.' I wagged my tail as he spoke, and when he'd finished fussing over me, walked to the patio doors which Ben then opened.

While Ben was making a cup of tea, I gave Aden a quick warning to stay where he was.

'Breakfast, Sandy,' Ben called, and I headed indoors and started eating. As soon as he grabbed his mug and made his way upstairs, I shot outside to get Aden. We shared my breakfast.

'Go the back way to Gina's house and stay close but out of sight until you see me.'

'WhereSandy? Howwill Iseeyou?'

74

'There's a tree between her house and one of her neighbours,' I said. 'Stay behind that tree and make sure you can see us but we can't see you. Be ready for me to come and fetch you. We won't have many chances, so you'll have to get into the van as quickly as you can. Got it, Aden?'

'YesFish.'

I heard the bedroom door close and Ben's voice. He was on his phone, I presumed, and I thought it must have been to Ellie.

'Go, Aden. Now!'

He disappeared and I could then hear from Ben's conversation that he wasn't talking to Ellie at all.

'No, I haven't seen Chip. It's unlikely he'd come here, I think... Okay, well good luck and if I do see him I'll let you know. I'm sure he'll turn up and will be just fine.'

He ended the call and looked at me. 'I hope Chip hasn't been taken like Obie and the others,' he muttered, half to himself.

I barked an, '*I do too, Ben,*' but Ben didn't speak dog so had no idea what I'd just said.

'All right, Sandy, I know you want your walk. Nearly ready.'

Unlike Ellie, when Ben said he was nearly ready, he meant it. He grabbed a few strange looking hats and an assortment of other items, put them in his rucksack, picked up his keys, packed drinks and a few treats for both humans and dogs, and closed the rucksack. He then put my lead on and we headed for Gina's, stopping on the way for a toilet break – for me, not Ben.

As we approached the house I glanced towards the tree but couldn't see Aden. I could only hope he was in place.

'Morning, Ben,' called Steve-the-Cheese as we approached the gate. 'Here's the keys to the van.' He threw them to Ben, who caught them. 'Put your kit in the back and leave the door open, get some air in there.'

Ben did as instructed, and, accompanied by a wag of my tail, I called a greeting to Bunty, Baxter, and Lexi.

'Where's Aden, old girl,' asked Bunty, and I discreetly nodded towards the tree.

The gate was left ajar as Ben went into the house, so I gave a low bark – the signal agreed with Aden – and he appeared within a few seconds. The van smelled of the perfume that came from the jar Ellie put above the sink in the bathroom, only in this small space it was ten times stronger. No wonder Steve wanted the door to be left open. The front section was partially cordoned off by a piece of thick board, but there were seats behind this and then a large cargo space. Aden jumped into the van, climbed over the seats and hunkered down onto the floor. If the men put anything into the back they wouldn't be able to see him and by the time he was discovered, it would be too late.

I rushed back to the garden. Shortly after, Ben and Steve appeared. They put blankets in the back for us to lie on and then we were off. As instructed by Bunty, Baxter and Lexi ignored Aden's presence, so as not to give the game away.

I found travelling boring, so closed my eyes and was soon asleep. I guess the others felt the same as I was the first to wake when we reached our destination.

Steve opened the back of the vehicle. 'Come on, you guys,' he said, shooshing us out with his hand. Bunty barked and Aden put his front paws up onto the seat and climbed over.

'What the...?'

'It's Chip,' said Ben, stating the obvious. 'How did he get here?'

'No idea.' Steve shooshed us out of the van so we could stretch our legs and answer any calls of nature required.

'Mike and Nicole are away and he escaped from the people he's staying with,' Ben said. 'They phoned me last night and said someone saw Sandy wandering around the early hours of this morning.'

Both men laughed. I gulped and turned my head away so they wouldn't be able to read my guilt. I could feel two pairs of eyes burning a hole in the back of my head and closed my own until I sensed they had looked away again.

'As if,' said Steve. 'Anyway, there's nothing we can do about it now. We'll just have to take him back later and explain that he jumped in the van without us knowing.'

'You're right. But isn't it strange that the other dogs didn't react to Chip's presence?'

'It's more than strange, Ben,' said Steve. 'I thought I understood dogs after working with them for so long, but I've never known anything like this to happen.'

We all sniffed the ground at the back of the vehicle, trying our best not to look interested in what they were saying. The back of my head was burning again.

'We can think about that later but for now we have to concentrate on the business in hand.'

As they talked they were taking items out of their bags and I was surprised to see Ben had brought Ellie's sunglasses and one of her hats.

I was utterly amazed when he pulled out something that looked like a deflated, blonde, Afghan Hound and slid it on top of his head. Blonde strands swung down past his shoulders – he almost looked like a female and I began to doubt myself, but his personal smell told me it was still Ben, even if he did look ridiculous. Bunty also shook her head in amazement. We watched, agog, as both men pulled on floppy hats and dark glasses.

'Slightly over the top, Ben,' Steve said.

'If this goes wrong and they're not put away after our visit today, we'll all be in even more danger than we are now.'

'Fair enough, whatever makes you happy. But you know you look like a plonker?'

Bunty let out a snort and the men looked at her.

'Coincidence,' said Ben, staring at us all.

I already knew they thought we were clever, but Steve trained dogs using commands and treats as rewards and refused to believe that any of us could understand every-day human conversations. I resisted the urge to wink or give him a smug look, knowing how confusing that could be for people who had shut their minds to our abilities. Instead, I yawned as if I was fed up with waiting and followed it up with a sigh. This took their attention off Bunty and they got back to the business at hand.

When they were kitted out, Steve took a moment to gather his thoughts and then said, 'So let me get this right, Ben, as we walk towards the compound, you want us to act like lovers on an afternoon stroll, even though nobody's about to see us?'

'Yup. Then you turn your back to the fence and pretend you're having a pee while I check out the surveillance cameras and disable them.'

'You know I'm convinced the cameras are just for show.'

'They might be, but if they're not we've covered all bases and they won't be able to identify us in this gear. And you did agree to it when we discussed the plan.'

'I know,' Steve looked down at his feet, then back up to Ben. 'But look at the state of us. This will go viral if we get caught and the cameras are working.' They both let out a laugh before turning serious again.

While all of us pretended to be bored or sleeping, secretly we were all listening intently.

'Okay, one more time,' said Steve. 'When you've disabled the cameras, or when we're sure they're not working, we bag your wig and the hats, you return and get Sandy and Baxter and leave Lola, Lexi, and Chip in the car to alert us if anyone approaches. Then, using one of the dogs as a diversion, the real work starts.'

'That's about it,' said Ben.

'Come on you lot, back in the van,' said Steve, ushering us in. As we duly obliged he whispered, 'Wish us luck,' then closed the door and turned to follow Ben.

Aden squeezed through the gap between the board and the side of the van and I followed. This enabled us to sit in the front so we could see out of the windscreen.

'Stay here, old boy,' Bunty said to Baxter, knowing he was too big to squeeze through the gap. Lexi stayed with Baxter as Bunty joined Aden and I in the front.

The three of us were now able to watch the men walking towards an area with a big building enclosed by a perimeter fence. The way Ben swung his bottom from side to side was like no woman I had ever seen walking and I voiced my opinion without thinking.

'Oh bless you, Fish,' said Bunty. 'You can be quite innocent.'

'What'sthatsupposedtomean?' Aden sat up panting.

'When some women want men to like them, old chap, that's how they choose to walk.'

'Seriously?' I had no idea what she was talking about and I could see Aden was none the wiser either. He squeezed back through the gap into the back of the van so he could spin a few times. We understood this was a way of dealing with pre-mission nerves, so Bunty let him be and we both tried to hide our irritation. Instead, we concentrated on what the men were doing.

They'd reached the perimeter fence and Ben sashayed off to the left while Steve faced towards us and unzipped his jeans. Less than a minute later, Ben ran towards Steve with his the Afghan Hound lookalike and the hat in his hand. I held my breath for a second as I watched two crazy dogs running along the inside of the fence. The men ignored them and, all business now, they both ran the short distance up the hill to where the van was parked. Bunty and I quickly joined the others in the back of the van where they'd left us.

'I told you they were working cameras,' said Ben.

'Okay, I was wrong. It has to be cannabis,' said Steve. 'They wouldn't have the cameras and savage guard dogs if it was just a warehouse.'

Ben gave a smug smile that swiftly turned serious. 'How long do you think we've got?'

'Well, if Sergeant Christo is true to his word, he will have arrested the twins and the police will arrive rather than the thugs.'

'You still want to go through with it?' asked Ben.

'Absolutely.' There was no hesitation in Steve's reply. 'I trust Sergeant Christo; but the twins, especially Yanni, have contacts in high places and I don't doubt that pressure's been put on Sergeant Christo and his family. I couldn't blame him if he caved at the last minute - that's why we have to do this. End it once and for all and show them they're not the only ones who can cause trouble. You know the consequences if we get caught, so you can wait here with Lola and Lexi if...'

'You know I'm in,' said Ben. 'If we don't act now, God only knows what they'll do next and I couldn't live with myself if something happened to one of my family.' He closed his eyes for a few seconds. 'Come on, let's go.'

Steve picked up the tranquiliser gun and carefully stored five darts.

'Stay, Lola and Lexi,' said Steve. 'Baxter, Sandy, come on.'

Aden started barking and spinning around - as much as he could in the space available in the van.

'And you, Chip,' Steve added.

'We can't take Chip,' said Ben. 'He's not ours to...'

'If anyone is in the area they'll hear that racket before seeing the van so we don't have a choice.'

'Damned if we do and damned if we don't,' said Ben as he let Aden out of the van.

Baxter started howling. Steve opened the van again without saying a word. Lexi jumped out and Baxter shut up. As we left, Bunty muttered a low 'Good luck team, make me proud.'

As we reached the fence there was no sign of the dogs, so Steve told Aden to run along the fenceline. It was exactly what Aden needed to calm him down, and it had the desired effect of luring out the two crazy guard dogs who went after him at full pelt. I was grateful there was a fence between them. I saw one other guard dog, and as I made ready to run the other way, Steve stopped me.

'Stay, Sandy.'

I did as I was told but took a step back as the deranged dog threw itself at the fence over and over again. Some of the words he shouted I'd heard the military men say in jest, but others sent shivers down my spine. No matter how many mad dogs I met, I would never get used to the violence and evil lurking beyond those eyes.

When the crazy dog questioned my parentage I let out a few low barks, 'You are a mad no-hoper and they're here to destroy you.'

He was shocked into stillness by my words, which gave Steve the ideal opportunity. The dart hit the dog in his side and within a few minutes he was sleeping like a puppy. Steve reloaded as Aden ran back towards us. He got the second dog but didn't have time to reload and aim at the other before the crazy ran away. Aden barked insults at the dog and I joined in.

'You mad dogs are too stupid to have a proper owner,' I shouted, but the crazy didn't reappear, and I was now starting to worry. There was no way Aden and I could fight this one and win, and Steve had already started to cut the wire. Perhaps we'd have a chance if Baxter joined in, but we couldn't be sure of his reactions, and so far he had watched without getting involved.

'Think you're tough then?' I barked.

Aden knew exactly where I was going with this. 'Come on then, Mr Champion Fighter, we're coming in - let's see what you're made of.'

'Or are you scared of us rescue dogs, now we have a big fella with us and a little fluffy dog...' I added.

'Fluffy dog?' Lexi raised an eyebrow, but she knew I was simply trying to wind up the crazy, so didn't take offence.

Our jeers did the trick and the crazy came bounding towards us, saliva swinging from its jowls.

'Please...' I offered a silent prayer as Steve aimed. It was a perfect shot and the crazy hit the deck with a yelp.

The tranquilizer darts had done their job and the three crazies were no longer barking but the silence seemed louder than the noise. It made me feel more uncomfortable than their ferocious growls and barking.

'It's okay, Sandy. You're safe and I won't let anyone or anything hurt you,' said Steve.

I remembered the dogs from Steve's shelter that had been massacred in the fire and knew he couldn't guarantee my safety. But his words, accompanied by the cheese he fished out of his pocket, did make me feel a little calmer. Steve had the knack of making you feel like the only dog in the world and I wondered if Baxter, Lexi and Aden felt the same as he spoke to them. I appreciated him taking the time to do this and was ready for whatever awaited us inside.

The hole in the fence was big enough for us dogs to get through and we waited as instructed until Ben and Steve squeezed in behind us and we all stood inside the lair of those evil men.

The building had large double doors secured by a number of locks that Ben and Steve couldn't break. We all ran around to the side of the building and Ben took something out of Steve's bag and used it to make a hole in the thin metal. When the hole was big enough, Ben shoved his hand through, eventually finding the handle and twisted it. He pulled the door open and the men walked into the building. We followed.

Inside, long, low tables running from one end of the room to the other, filled the space. The tops of the tables were filled with strange smelling plants, each lit and heated by artifical lights which blazed down. I had no idea what the plants were but I didn't like their smell. Above the sound of our men talking together I heard another noise, and from the look on Aden's face, I knew he'd heard it too. Ben wasted no time and started to throw a smelly liquid on some of the plants.

'I'll start at the other end,' said Steve.

I had a flashback to the fire in the woods, then to the conversation between Ben and Ellie about the fire in Steve's other rescue centre. I barked and it sounded too loud in the silence of the warehouse.

'What is it, Sandy?'

Before I could say anything else, Aden, Lexi, and Baxter started running towards the sound we'd heard and I followed. When the men failed to follow us, I stopped and trotted back to Ben. Aden was now barking constantly but I ignored him, barked once at Ben, turned and jogged towards Aden, then looked around pointedly at both Ben and Steve.

'Okay, we're coming,' said Ben.

As we all neared the far end of the building, a smell of fear, neglect, and illness became apparent. Steve said nothing about the smell but he could now hear the muted barks and yelping.

'Ben, there's dogs behind that door!' He pointed to his left.

As expected, the door was locked. I barked a warning for the occupants to move back as Steve kicked the door. After a few attempts, it splintered and swung open. A number of young dogs lay about the room too weak to move; I'm not sure how many there were because I was distracted by a voice I recognised.

'Sandeeee!'

Obie was sprawled in a corner. He was emaciated, his bones showed through his skin and scabs covered his body. Instead of having clear, healthy eyes, his were bloodshot. Despite this, he managed to thump his tail gently when he saw us.

'For the love of Lassie!' I ran over and greeted him with licks and kisses. 'We'll get you out of here, Obie. You're coming home.'

'What'shappened? Whathavetheydonetoyou? Willhebeallright?' Aden fired questions until Steve told him to calm down, then he came over to greet Obie.

'Look at the state of these poor animals,' said Steve, trying not to heave at the smell. 'The depths of human cruelty never ceases to amaze me.'

He had stopped gagging but his face had changed colour and I believed he was trying his best not to puke. I dragged my eyes away from Obie and had a proper look around.

There must have been nearly thirty dogs there, and by the look of it, they had been forced to do everything in this room. Faeces was in one corner and empty food and water bowls in another. I noticed a small Pekinese who was barely breathing. What was left of his coat was infested and the skin that was showing was covered in scabs.

'Poor Bonzo's in a bad way,' said Obie. 'I hope it's not too late.'

'We'll get you back home to your people parents,' I said to the puppy before licking his face. 'It's going to be okay.' I was trying to convince myself as well as Bonzo, but knew it would be touch and go.

'Right, this changes everything,' said Steve. 'We need to get these to the van before we destroy this business once and for all. But I want some photos first.'

Ben dug his phone out of his pocket.

'Be quick-I don't want to prolong their agony any more than I have to.'

Ben had already started taking photos from different parts of the room. He talked as he snapped away. 'If we set it on fire we destroy the evidence and there's even less chance of a prosecution.'

'There's more than one way to skin a cat, Ben. We've got work to do, come on.'

The phone went back in Ben's pocket, and they now moved quickly. I had known almost as soon as I met Ben, that he was used to being in charge but for the sake of speed he seemed happy to do as Steve said. Their priority –

and ours – was to get the dogs out of this stinking hell-hole. Obie explained that the dogs being held for ransom were kept in the disgusting room, the rest were used for hunting then more or less forgotten about when the twins and their hunting cronies had no use for them. Occasionally a lump of meat or salad waste was thrown into the room and the water bowls filled, but this was random and the dogs were always hungry and thirsty. Dogs that couldn't keep up on the hunt due to starvation or exhaustion were either left behind, or brought back and killed by the crazies, as sport for the entertainment of the hunting party.

'I thought that was going to happen to meeee,' said Obie, 'but Yanni wanted to see what I was like at tracking and hunting so I worked my paws off so I could literally save my own lifeee. I heard them talk about asking Gina for money too.'

'The rotten bounders,' said Baxter. 'The horrible twins must be planning on blackmailing her as well. Let's get out of here before anyone returns.'

Steve and Ben carried those who were unable to walk the short distance up the hill towards the van. The rest slowly followed and I could see it was a major effort for them to drag themselves up the scree-covered incline. Aden and I dragged Obie and encouraged him with stories from home when he looked like he couldn't put one paw in front of another.

As we approached the van I heard a warning bark from Bunty. I left Obie and rushed toward Ben to warn him, but it was too late.

A shot went off and that sound of gunfire initially silenced us all for a nano-second - then all hell was let loose. Most of the dogs we were trying to save, panicked. Those that could, ran back down the hill in the direction of the building.

A man appeared from behind the van. He was pointing his shotgun at Steve.

Baxter growled. 'I'm not going to let him hurt our pack.'

'It's going to be all right, he won't hurt us.' Lexi replied.

I knew she was just trying to reassure Baxter and resisted stating the obvious about where his gun was pointing.

'You swines come here and threaten my family and think I'll let you get away with it?' he said in heavy accented English as he took a few steps closer to our group. 'Well you're not going to get away with it.'

'The police are on their way,' Ben said calmly, but either the man didn't hear or refused to listen. He took a breath and I knew without a doubt he was about to fire the weapon. We were all rooted to the ground and my world went into slow motion.

'Noooooooo,' barked Lexi as she sensed Baxter about to move.

'I'm tired of being a victim,' Baxter growled at the same time as he leapt through the air towards the man. But the gun had gone off. Lexi yelped and was then silent. The quiet worried me more than her yelping. I didn't have time to think it through as the sound of another shot rang out and Steve hit the deck.

Baxter flew through the air, hitting the man before he could reload his gun. The weapon flew out of his hand and he was pinned to the ground, Baxter's weight totally incapacitating him. He growled ferociously and a wet patch appeared on the man's jeans.

'Don't kill him,' Lexi barked from where she lay on the ground. 'They'll destroy you and I don't want to be on my own.'

I took a breath, relieved that the little Maltese was well enough to speak.

'I ought to kill him after what he's done to you,' Baxter growled.

'I'm all right, it's only a graze and I'll be a bit sore from the fall, but the bullet glanced off me.'

'I should kill him for shooting Steve,' Baxter replied, '...but I won't, and he doesn't know that.' Ensuring his body still held the man prone, he leaned his face over that of his captive and snarled directly into his eyes. His slobber landed on the man's nose and dripped onto his chin. The former aggressor started wailing in his native tongue.

While this was going on, Ben had removed his t-shirt and was using it to apply pressure to Steve's shoulder, where the bullet had hit.

'How is it, if that's not a stupid question?' he asked.

Steve bit his bottom lip. 'It could have been worse but I need to get to the hospital before I lose too much blood. How's Lexi? Is she going to be okay?'

Although spoken as a matter of fact, Steve's face had whitened and I could see he was in pain, but it was typical of Steve-the-Cheese to show concern for one of his four-legged family, even through his own agony.

'She's moving about so she must be okay, but I'll check once we get you sorted. Can you maintain the pressure while I phone for an ambulance?'

As they spoke, they were both ignoring the cries of the man whom Baxter was detaining and, one by one, the other dogs returned, sensing they were no longer in danger. Most sat quietly around our small group but a few sat with Lexi, licking and reassuring her. Despite her attempt at bravado, and her reassurances to Baxter, Lexi started to shake. I ran over to her and gave her the once over. My inspection confirmed what she'd told Baxter, and I sighed with relief knowing that she was going to be okay.

Ben started to make the call but stopped to turn at the sound of sirens approaching in the distance. The police arrived shortly after; Sergeant Christo with an unknown police constable. We watched the new man patch Steve up as best he could before the ambulance arrived.

'Where's your regular constable,' asked Ben.

'Under arrest,' Sergeant Christo replied, 'for corruption and attempted bribery.'

'What the... ah, that hurts,' Steve said, clearly in pain. The ambulance arrived and unloaded a man and woman who were both dressed in green scrubs. They took various items out of their daily carry bags and one of them injected something into Steve's arm which seemed to calm him down. He looked like he was in less pain within seconds and he started muttering to Ben.

'Look after Baxter and get Lexi to the vet. Don't let anyone take Baxter away for what he's done,' he said, as they stretchered him into the ambulance. 'Tell Gina I'm okay. Don't let her worry about me.'

'Will do, but don't worry about anything. I'll look after things. Just take care and we'll come to see you as soon as we can.'

'I forgot,' Steve said, as the paramedic made sure his cot was secure prior to whisking him off to hospital. 'Gina-tell Gina I love her...' His eyes closed and so did the ambulance door.

'Now let's deal with this one,' Sergeant Christo said. He hadn't appeared to be in much of a hurry to get Baxter off the horrible man who had eventually stopped shouting and was now lying quietly beneath the big dog.

Baxter seemed quite content to stay where he was as the policemen approached. They weren't sure about the big dog, so Ben called him. Baxter shook his head, purposely dribbling over the man before moving.

'I'm going to get my lawyers onto you,' the man shouted at Ben.

'You're under arrest,' said Sergeant Christo. 'Cuff him,' he nodded to the PC.

'*I'm* under arrest? You should charge this foreign scum with breaking and entering. I was only defending my property...' he kept going on and on, until Baxter growled again, catching his attention. The man went quiet so Sergeant Christo read him his rights and manoeuvred him into the back of the police car alongside the PC. He then went to ask Ben to round us up.

'Digger, old chap,' Bunty beamed as soon as the van was opened. She jumped out and they ran around each other, nuzzling like two puppies at play. 'How absolutely marvellous to see you!' We'll spoil you and soon have you back to your usual self, boy. Laura and Greg will be delighted to see you and Gina will be over the moon!'

In my mind, with the mission now over, I reverted back to our day-to-day names and watched as Lola made a big fuss of Obie. Although he looked happy, I could see that he was still tense – his eyes darted from side to side and I knew his nightmare wouldn't be over until we were far away from this living hell. In fact, knowing Obie as I did, I wasn't sure if he would ever recover from this. I knew that now the mission was over, Lola would have to use all of her skills to counsel him in an attempt for him to find his former self.

It seemed to me that some people were pure evil and I silently thanked the lord of dogs for putting us in the care of Ben, Ellie, Gina, and Steve-the-Cheese, and for the help of Sergeant Christo, all of whom were the polar opposites of the vicious and evil twins and the man now ranting in the back of the police car.

As Ben and Sergeant Christo chatted, Lola clearly didn't think the mission was over and started giving orders. She could see how restless Obie and Chip had become.

'Aden,' she said, 'while I talk to Digger, I want you to make these poor souls as comfortable as you can under the circumstances.'

Chapter 8

It was a tight squeeze in the van on the way back. Sergeant Christo had agreed that Ben could take the rescued dogs to Steve's newly built centre and he should report to the police station early the following morning to give a statement.

'I'll speak to my bosses but there's no guarantee you and Steve won't be charged for trespass and breaking and entering.'

'And for saving a number of dogs from certain death,' added Ben, 'some of whom had been dognapped and their owners were being blackmailed.'

'I'm not unsympathetic, but it's out of my hands,' said Sergeant Christo. 'I'll arrange for the owners to be contacted later today and I'll warn Panni to expect some visitors at the rescue centre. Now go on, you look done-in.' He put one arm around Ben's shoulder and held out his other. The men shook hands and Ben gave a wry smile.

'We were trying to do the right thing and to protect our loved ones.'

'And I would have done exactly the same,' said Sergeant Christo. 'Are you all right to drive back?'

'Yeah, I'll be fine,' Ben replied.

'Try to get a good night's sleep tonight and don't worry about Steve. He's in good hands and he'll be okay.'

They said their goodbyes, Ben closed the van, started the engine and off we went.

Ben listened to sad music on the radio during the drive home and we kept quiet for most of the journey, except when more than one of us tried to move which caused a domino effect and general chaos amongst the rest of us. The Pekinese puppy lay perfectly still and I worried about him.

It was dark by the time we arrived at the centre to be greeted by Panni.

'Hi Ben, how's Steve? I hope those scumbags go down for a very long time.'

'He was in pain when I left him, Panni. But he'll be fine. Do you think the dogs will be safe here?'

'Most definitely,' Panni responded and a slow smile spread over his face. 'I take it you haven't heard?'

Ben had now opened the back door of the van and two of the volunteers arrived to start taking the dogs into the centre. He handed Lexi to one of them.

'This brave little lady's been shot at today. Can you get the vet to check her over?' Ben said, turning his attention back to Panni who was grinning. 'Come on, mate. Put me out of my misery,' he said, clearly confused at Panni's change of attitude.

'Events have moved on in the two hours since you've been driving back. My cousin phoned with news. It was the twins' great uncle who shot Steve, and he's been charged.'

'I know, Panni. That happened when we were there,' Ben said wearily.

'Well what you don't know, is that both twins have been taken into custody. Michaelis tried to bribe the Environment and Agriculture Minister.'

'Yeah, right,' said Ben. 'And how would your cousin know this?'

Panni ignored his scepticism. 'My cousin is a lawyer and has connections. More importantly, his wife is the Justice Minister's top aide. She's told him a public statement by the minister will be released within the next twenty-four hours, signalling a crackdown on bribery and corruption. Looks like they're going to make an example of the Savvidis twins.'

'About time too.'

'You don't get it, do you, Ben? Sergeant Christo and brave men like him, have been trying to do this for years. The twins aren't the only ones who try to bribe those in power. This is a massive deal for the majority of the people here who are honest and hard-working. We've won, Ben. We've flaming well won!' In a rare moment of emotion, Panni grabbed hold of Ben and gave him a big man-hug. When they pulled apart, they high-fived and then both started laughing.

Baxter gave a celebratory bark and Obie joined in. Chip did a little spin and Lola gave me a *'What the heck?'* look as she joined in, too. I couldn't help myself and neither could the new dogs who had just been taken into the centre- we all either barked or howled happily. If they hadn't already, the rescued dogs now sensed their nightmare was over. It was a joyous sound, but deafening.

Ben and Panni looked at each other in confusion before taking action and telling us all to calm down and be quiet.

'What was all that about?' Panni asked.

Ben shrugged his shoulders. 'Perhaps they picked up on our moods.'

'Yeah, maybe.' The initial euphoria now over, Panni continued, 'As I was saying, as well as the bribery and corruption, there'll be the charges of possessing a cannabis farm, growing and selling the plants, possibly money laundering and also the cruelty to animals. Other criminals will be shaking in their boots when they discover what's happened but I suspect the crackdown has already begun. That's why Sergeant Christo got to you before you had a chance to phone for the police.'

'How do you know that? I didn't mention...'

'I have contacts, Ben. That's one thing that will never change on this island.'

'All the dogs are in and settled,' one of the other volunteers came to tell Panni. 'The vet's checking them all over now and he needs to talk to you; and one of the owners has phoned to say he's on his way.'

Panni said a hasty goodbye, with Ben agreeing that he'd update him on Steve's condition the following day, 'If Steve doesn't phone you first,' he finished.

The mood was lighter in the car on the short ride home from the rescue centre, and there was certainly more room in the back with only me, Lola, Obie, Baxter, Lexi, and Chip remaining.

'Let's get you home first, Chip,' Ben leaned over and gave him a head rub. 'Then we'll get the rest of you organised at my place.'

Chip attempted a few spins but gave a gentle bark and lay down quickly when the van started moving.

Ben took a deep breath when we arrived at Nicole and Mike's home. He opened the back door and quickly closed it after Chip jumped out.

'Go see what's happening,' Lola said to me, so I jumped over the seats to watch out of the side window. I couldn't hear anything except for Chip barking, and saw that Ben looked embarrassed as he was speaking. Then the vibe changed. Nicole threw herself at Ben with such force that he had to step back. I thought she was going to squeeze the breath out of him as she hugged him.

'Well that went better than expected,' he muttered as he got back into the car and drove the short distance to our home. 'Come on you lot.' Ben parked up and we all jumped out, headed up the drive and waited by the front door. Seeing he was on his phone, the other dogs made themselves comfortable outside. But I smelled something very exciting and couldn't keep still.

'Panni? Yes, it's me, Ben. Remember the miniature poodle I dropped off? Has the vet given her the okay yet?'

We listened while Ben waited for an answer.

'Great. He belongs to friends of Chip's folks, Nicole and Mike. They said they might know who some of the other dogs belong to as well if all the owner's haven't already been found.' He hesitated again while listening to whatever Panni was saying. 'Okay, I'll ask them to call you.'

'What's wrong, Sandy? What is it?' he asked as soon as he put his phone away.

I was in a frenzy by this stage. The other dogs had now smelled what I had and knowing how happy I was, their tails were wagging furiously, too.

103

'For the love of Lassie! Open the door!' I barked. I stared pointedly at it, then back to Ben, who frowned but got it-it still seemed like an age before he fished out his keys and did so.

'Surprise!' Two voices called out.

Ellie threw herself at Ben and I leapt up onto Mia. The force of my enthusiasm knocked her onto the floor and I covered her face in big licks to show her how good it was to see her.

'I've missed you too, Sandy. I love you, you know.' She giggled as I showed her how glad I was to see her. Despite my enthusiasm, I could feel eyes on my back. I stopped and turned around. Ellie and Ben were now standing next to each other, smiling down at me and Mia. Ellie had been busy so I'd welcomed Mia first, but now it was time to show her how glad I was that she was home. I gave a gentle bark and threw myself at my second favourite person, with the same enthusiasm I had for Mia. Ellie was strong but so was I. When I hit her with the force of all my body, she somehow managed to catch me in her arms without falling over. I was taken aback and turned my head to one side in astonishment.

'I've been working out, Sandy,' she said, burying her head in my fur and muttering sweet nothings. I loved her scent, her voice, her warmth...just about everything about her, and nestled happily on her chest as she carried me to the settee. She sat down, still cuddling me, seemingly forgetting about the other people and dogs in the room.

'Aw, who's this?' asked Mia. 'She's soooo cute.'

I knew without looking that she was talking about Lexi. While Ellie was still stroking me, I sneaked a peek at Mia who was picking Lexi up and ignoring the other dogs. Aside from Lola, who rolled her eyes at me, the others didn't seem to mind.

'Remember me?' asked Ben, and Ellie laughed.

'Come and join us,' she said, patting the seat beside us. He was over in a flash.

I was in heaven until Obie decided enough was enough and jumped onto the settee. Baxter almost suffocated us all by joining in the fun and Mia lifted Lexi up so she didn't feel left out. It was both fun and funny and my people giggled as we all barked, fighting for their attention.

'Gina's gone straight to the hospital with the kids,' Ellie said in a moment of calm. 'We'll look after the dogs tonight, then try to get back to normal tomorrow.'

I looked around at my favourite people and four-legged friends. I was in doggie heaven and happy to stay this way forever.

Who needed normal anyway?

Epilogue

It was the grand opening of Steve's new rescue centre, *Dogs for Life*. I knew it was a very special day as Ellie had taken me to the spa the day before and everyone who stroked me told me how wonderful I smelled, how beautiful I looked, and how soft my fur was. I wasn't alone, as the other squad members had also been taken, along with Baxter and Lexi, the latter now fully recovered from the physical injuries received at the illegal farm.

I looked around at both my dog and people friends. Steve-the-Cheese was no longer wearing the bandage around his arm and shoulder and he was talking to Panni and Barry; the other volunteers were standing behind them. Ben, Ellie, and Gina were in their own little group with Mike and Nicole who were trying to keep Chip still. Ellie was talking to Gina, who wasn't really paying attention because every now and then she looked towards Steve. Lola sat quietly at Gina's feet-she was looking around at the guests and I wondered what was going through her mind. She must have sensed me looking as she winked when our eyes made contact.

Young Greg and Mia were holding hands and Greg was holding Obie's lead with in his other hand. I was standing next to Mia. Obie was the only one of us on a lead

– I thought Gina would have known by now that he would never run away again, but I suppose it stopped her from worrying.

Laura was standing to the left of her mother, accompanied by her friend Katie. Laura was holding Lexi and both girls were fussing over her. Lexi was revelling in the attention. Baxter sat quietly at their feet and was happy to get a bit of attention now and then from Katie.

The dogs who had been taken were there with their people parents, except for the young Pekinese, Bonzo, who had been too weak to save and had died on his first night at the centre. The only consolation was that he'd had love and kindness showered upon him in his final hours and had died a free dog. His owner hadn't been found until the following day and was understandably devastated at the news of his death. Unfortunately, she was one of the people who had sent the requested money to the twins in the hope that Bonzo would be returned unharmed. She stood near the front of the gathered audience.

Steve clapped his hands to get everyone's attention, then spoke into a loud speaker so that we could all hear.

'Hello everyone. Welcome to the grand opening of our new rescue centre, *Dogs for Life*. I'm sorry to have to start the proceedings with bad news but out of the twenty-eight dogs we rescued from that horrendous farm, one didn't make it. Bonzo, the Pekinese puppy, was just too weak. Despite our best efforts, he died the morning after being rescued. Poor Mrs Kyriakis was devastated at the news and will never forget Bonzo.'

A sympathetic murmur spread throughout the audience and everyone paused for a moment to remember Bonzo, and console Mrs Kyriakis.

'But she's keen to give a needy dog a home and has asked to adopt one of the other dogs we rescued.' Steve stopped for a moment, and right on cue, Panni appeared behind him with a small, young, dog that looked similar to Obie, except he was completely black. 'Mrs Kyriakis and Tiger have already visited together and get along just fine. Mrs Kyriakis?'

The sprightly older lady hurried forward and took Tiger from Panni's arms. He wriggled in delight and covered her with big licks.

'I think this is a match made in heaven,' Steve said. Mrs Kyriakis thanked him and made her way back into the crowd. Tiger was still wriggling so she put him down so he could have a good sniff around.

'Seven of the remaining twenty-six dogs have been reunited with their owners, five of whom are with us today. Ladies and gentlemen?'

The people parents of the missing dogs put up their hands or nodded and the crowd clapped politely, some bending down to stroke and cuddle the dogs. The couple Chip had stayed with looked relaxed and happy now they were reunited with their own four-legged friend.

'Of the remaining nineteen, two have been taken to a specialist vet and are progressing well, though I'm told it will be a while before they're back to full health. I'm delighted to report that we have already found forever homes for another eleven in the UK and Germany. So the remaining six dogs are currently in the centre, together with another three, older, puppies who were dumped here this morning. We can house a maximum of sixty-two dogs at a push, providing we have the funds. As well as today being our official opening, you know we're a charity so we hope to raise as much money as possible to enable us to give proper care to the dogs that are left here, for whatever reason.'

Steve stopped for a minute as we all heard the sound of four by four vehicles pulling up.

'It's the mayor!' Ellie sounded surprised as she whispered to Ben. 'I wonder what he's done with his flash car?'

'Mukhtar,' Ben said.

Ellie looked at Gina and raised her eyebrows.

'I saw that,' said Ben. 'All Mukhtars have had to give up their expensive cars and get something more practical. It's all part of this corruption crack down and the government wants to make savings centrally and locally.'

'I wonder who's in the other one?'

'I've seen him on the telly,' said Ben. 'He's the Minister for the Environment, Fisheries and Farms or something like that.'

We all watched as the visitors shook hands with Steve and his staff.

'Ladies, gentlemen and dogs,' said the Mukhtar.

The people chuckled but I failed to get the joke. Looking around I could see my doggy friends didn't get it either.

'Steve and Panni, and their many volunteers, have made a fantastic contribution to our island. I wish we didn't have to have animal rescue centres but the sad fact of life is that we do, and Steve and his team do a wonderful job of looking after these poor unfortunate dogs, as well as educating as many people as they can about good animal husbandry. I now pronounce *Dogs for Life* officially open.' He turned to Steve and his team and started to clap. The audience joined in and Steve and his team looked on awkwardly. Then Steve passed the Mukhtar a pair of scissors, and he cut the tape that was loosely tied to the front door.

The crowd cheered and the Mukhtar waited for the noise to die down before continuing his speech, 'You will all have heard about the devastating fire that killed a number of dogs and destroyed Steve's last rescue centre. The twins responsible have recently started a long stretch in prison, for that and their many other crimes. If it wasn't for the bravery of some members of our police force, as well as a few civilians and their dogs, these men and other members of their gang would still be free to cause misery and chaos to the lives of many people and animals. So today isn't only about opening the centre. Minister Chloros has kindly agreed to make some special presentations. Sir?'

The minister stepped forward. 'Ladies and gentlemen, I echo everything said by the Mukhtar. On behalf of the president, I would like to present the Island Order of Merit to the following individuals... Steve Nicolaou.'

The look of surprise on Steve-the-Cheese's face was an absolute picture, and so was that of Ben's when he was called up next. Sergeant Christo followed, then Panni and the men looked more embarrassed than proud as the medals were also pinned to their chests and everyone clapped and cheered.

'The contribution of a number of brave dogs has also been recognised and the President has authorised the award of the Purple Island Order of Merit to Lola, Sandy, Chip, Baxter, and Lexi for their help in saving many human and dog's lives, and for Obie who has endured dognapping twice.'

Now it was our turn to look surprised as Gina headed to the front with Lola and the rest of us followed with our respective people.

As the audience clapped and cheered I looked at my friends. It would take time for Obie, Baxter, and Lexi's emotional scars to heal, but I knew without a shadow of doubt that they'd receive the same love and kindness that I'd been fortunate to have from Ben and Ellie. Eventually their nightmares would lessen and they'd be happy dogs again. Chip was as restless as usual-and as for Lola? Well, she sidled over to me as the minister started to pin rosettes onto the collars of our other friends. 'Enjoy yourself today, Fish old girl,' she whispered. 'But never forget that duty comes first. We may have won this battle, but the next injustice could be right around the corner and the dog squad must be ready.'

It was a sobering thought indeed, but I was sure a few treats would put it to the back of my mind and lighten my mood.

Acknowledgements

Thanks to my husband Allan for listening (or doing a good job of pretending to listen) and to the real Sandy for inspiring this series. Thanks also to my awesome editor Jill Turner, to Jessica Bell for another fantastic cover, to my friends Trudy Eitschberger, Julie Woodruff, Su Echo Falls S'ari and Charity Rowell, and to all my other friends and readers for your support.

Author's Note

Thank you for purchasing this book. I hope you enjoyed reading about the dog squad as much as I enjoyed writing about them. Any reviews are gratefully received – I love reading them all.

If you like what you've read so far, you may be interested in my other books:

Beyond Death (The Afterlife Series Book 1)
Beyond Life (The Afterlife Series Book 2)
Beyond Destiny (The Afterlife Series Book 3)
Beyond Possession (The Afterlife Series Book 4)

Unlikely Soldiers Book 1 (Civvy to Squaddie)
Unlikely Soldiers Book 2 (Secrets and Lies)
Unlikely Soldiers Book 3 (Friends and Revenge)

Court Out (A Netball Girls' Drama)

And for children:

Jason the Penguin (He's Different)
Jason the Penguin (He Learns to Swim)

Further information is on my website https://debmcewansbooksandblogs.com or you can connect with me on Facebook: https://www.facebook.com/DebMcEwansbooksandblogs/?ref=bookmarks

About the Author

Following a career of over thirty years in the British Army, Deb and her husband moved to Cyprus to become weather refugees.

She's written children's books about Jason the penguin and Barry the reindeer and young adult/adult books about dogs, the afterlife, soldiers, and netball players.

The first book in the Unlikely Soldiers series is set in nineteen-seventies Britain. The second covers the early eighties and includes the Falklands War, service in Northern Ireland and (the former) West Germany. 'Friends and Revenge' is the third in the series, and takes a sinister turn of events.

'Court Out (A Netball Girls' Drama)' is Deb's latest standalone novel. Using netball as an escape from her

miserable home life, Marsha Lawson is desperate to keep the past buried and to forge a brighter future. But she's not the only one with secrets. When two players want revenge, a tsunami of emotions is released at a tournament, leaving destruction in its wake. As the wave starts spreading throughout the team, can Marsha and the others escape its deadly grasp, or will their emotional baggage pull them under,
with devastating consequences for their families and teammates?

The Afterlife series was inspired by ants. Deb was in the garden contemplating whether to squash an irritating ant or to let it live. She wondered whether anyone *up there* decides the same about us and thus the series was born.

'The Island Dog Squad' is a series of novellas inspired by the rescue dog Deb and Allan adopted this March. The real Sandy is a sensitive soul, not quite like her fictional namesake, and the other characters are based on Sandy's real-life mates.

Deb loves spending time with her husband Allan and rescue dog Sandy. She also loves writing, keeping fit, and socialising, and does her best to avoid housework.

Printed in Poland
by Amazon Fulfillment
Poland Sp. z o.o., Wrocław